Daddy's Curse 3

The Birth of A Monster

Luke. G. Dahl

BASED ON TRUE EVENTS

This is a work of non-fiction. I have tried to recreate events, locales and

conversations from everyone involved. In order to maintain their

anonymity in some instances I have changed the names of individuals and

places, I may have changed some identifying characteristics and details

such as physical properties, occupations and places of residence.

DADDY'S CURSE 3: THE BIRTH OF A MONSTER

This book is only to try to create awareness to these tragedies so they

can be stopped. No one involved in the creation of this book in any

way approves or supports this sort of harrowing deeds

It contains strong language, explicit violence and scenes of a sexual

nature

Editing by Stephanie Hoogstad

Designed by Rebecacovers

Beautiful minds inspire others

Written by Luke. G. Dahl.

First edition. December 1, 2018.

Contents

PROLOGUE

My father once told me a story, a story rooted in Greek mythos. It was the story of Icarus, the boy who flew to close to the sun. Icarus was aided by his father, who concocted a pair of wings that would enable him to fly. Icarus was elated and wanted to take the wings for a test drive, an act his father allowed.

"But," my father noted, looking straight into my eyes with his piercing brown eyes, "Daedalus warned his son, Icarus, not to go too close to the sun or too low into the sea. However, Icarus didn't listen and flew higher and higher until he went too close to the sun," my father continued. "Do you know what happened to Icarus?"

I shook my head to signify my answer was a no.

"He died," Father said bluntly, sending shivers down my spine. He placed his hands on my shoulders firmly with my mother watching from the background, a terrified look on her face. I remember wondering why Mother was so scared. I would find out soon enough. "Bat, what do you think the moral of this story is?" Even at such a young age, I could tell he was angry for some reason. It was getting easier and easier to tell.

"Always obey your parents?" I answered it as a question, which made him furrow his brows even more.

"I didn't hear you." He raised his voice and I answered with more assertiveness this time.

"Good," Father mused. "Obedience. Order. Submission. If you want to succeed in life, Bat, you must make people submit and obey your will, and you must also obey the will of others above you." He walked over to my mother, who looked like she was going to die.

"And when they disobey your will..." he chimed as my mother shook her head vehemently, already crying and rubbing her hands together as an attempt to plead with him.

"You punish them," he simply stated before landing a hot slap on my mother's face that sent her staggering backward and clutching the swollen area.

"Please, please, Chuluun. I beg—"

Her pleas were cut short as he grabbed her throat and jammed her head against the wall, causing her to groan and try to claw his larger, stronger hand with her little ones to no avail.

"If you obey, you will be given anything you want!" he barked, slapping her face with the back of his hand.

"Follow me, Bat!" my father ordered, and I complied. He dragged my mother by the hair from my room to theirs, kicking her along the way while all she could do was writhe and wiggle in pain, screaming for every kick he gave her and groaning all the way.

"This...Is...How...You...Command...Respect!!"Father shouted with a slap, kick or punch for each word he emphasized. I just stood there, confused, scared and shocked. Was this really how to command respect and obedience from people? I stood still, barely blinking and only flinching when he gave her hard hits. Father beat Mother to his satisfaction that day, and after he was done, he ordered Mother to clean *the shit* up, referring to her blood, before walking away and going down the stairs. I quietly walked to the bathroom and got a towel prior to pouring water in a bowl then went to where my mother remained, sprawled upon the floor in her own blood. I helped her up and cleaned her nose, which kept seeping out blood. I cleaned her up and cleaned the room while she rested.

"You are a good son, Bat," my mother chimed as I was about walking away.

"You are an even better mother," I replied before leaving.

I was eight years old then, and that was the last time my father and I really talked about any issue until my teenage years. This was the life I grew up in.

CHAPTER ONE

THE ERDENES

"Good morning, Ming," I said as Ming opened the gate for the driver to take me to school. Ming was my favorite employee on Father's payroll. He had been like a father to me all these years and my confidant. Father had gone to Mongolia on business as he frequently did, and my mother always seemed to relish the absence. The only problem for her was the guards watching her and the house around the clock in an attempt by my father to keep her under control. Not that she was doing anything anyways, but that was the way my father was. He always wanted to be in control and know what everyone was doing. He was a very powerful man, and that attracted enemies, which made him even more paranoid.

"How are you, Bat?" Ming responded while opening the gate.

"I'm good. Bye." I waved to him before getting into the car.

As I was driven to school, I looked through the window as I did every time I was taken out. We lived in Chengdu, China, which was the capital of the Sichuan Province. It was one of China's most populous cities, but it was more serene than the other big cities, having a quieter disposition. The city was well known for its lower levels of heat compared to other parts of Eastern China and instead had regular rainfall, especially in the months of June and July. This gave Chengdu a gloomy look in my eyes a lot of the time. On the plus side, the city, especially the area in which we lived, had a strong sense of community despite the population, with a lot of people know one another. I looked on as people drenched in filth sat down by the walkways, begging for scraps and change from people walking by. I chuckled as I watched numerous numbers of them.

"What's funny, Mr. Bat?" Li, the driver, asked. Even though I wasn't as close with Li as I was with Ming, he and I were still friendly enough to engage in casual talks on the way to school every day of the week. He was a tall, lanky man with a chatty nature. He just loved to talk and engage in a lot of conversations. He always said "seeing the world from another person's eyes increases one's knowledge", which I agreed with.

"Oh, nothing," I said casually. "Just looking at these peasants begging for food makes me laugh." I scoffed. He didn't reply. I wondered why but decided not to stress the matter.

My school was an English-speaking school. Most rich parents in Chengdu already felt their children knew Chinese but needed to learn English since it was a more significant language in the world at that point in time, especially in foreign trade. The school was not too far from my home. One would be able to walk there on foot, but it was a school for the elite, with each parent trying to one-up the other. This meant I was always to be driven to and from school no matter what, and that was how it was supposed to be. I shouldn't be walking the streets like a lowlife. I was an Erdene, and like Father always said, some names are worth more than others.

Li dropped me off and we waved goodbye to each other before I departed into the building. Unlike most of my mates, I loved school. Father had ingrained in me that to be successful in life, one had to have knowledge. This spurred me to take education incredibly seriously, reading books and speaking diction well beyond my years. I was eleven years by now but used words that would have made people think I was much older. Yang and Yie, my two best friends, ran to me.

"Good morning, Bat," Yang said with an innocent smile. He was an incredibly beautiful and feminine-looking boy, quite gullible and easy to manipulate, which was why he needed me to protect him. He did what I asked and obeyed, which was why I had a closer relationship with him than Yie, who also obeyed but liked to test the boundaries of my patience.

"Good morning, Yang," I said, giving him my bag, which he happily took from my hands. I looked at Yie, expecting him to greet me. He had already hesitated, which was why I gave him the stern look.

"Good morning, Bat," Yie said with a mischievous smile. I was sure he just wanted to get me in a bad mood. That was how he was, but he remained my friend because he was fiercely loyal to me. He was the biggest of the three of us and one of the tallest in our grade. This was why I wanted him as my friend in the first place, he was very useful as muscle when I wanted to get what I wanted from someone and couldn't talk them into or out of it.

I didn't reply to him and just walked to class. Being the best student and one of the richest, if not the richest, I was incredibly popular. Both boys and girls wanted to be my friends, and they should. I was better than all of them. My teachers, however, didn't like me too much because, according to them, my attitude was not exemplary. I surmised they were just jealous because their lives probably did not turn out the way they wished and were now taking it out on me. One such teacher was Mrs. Qiu, our mathematics teacher.

In the class that day, I had already read the topic she was teaching, which made it boring to sit and listen to. I began reading another book I had in my bag to pass away the time.

"Master Bat," I heard my name being called after a few minutes and looked up. Mrs. Qiu was scowling at me, her large glasses resting on her nose.

"Do you mind sharing with us the answer to the question?" she asked me, the scowl still plastered on her face.

"Not really," I retorted, prompting a few chuckles here and there from the rest of the class. She smiled at me sarcastically, but it disappeared as fast as it came.

"Answer the question, Bat Erdene," she ordered in her stern voice.

"I don't even know the question, Mrs. Qiu," I confessed. What was she going to do? Teachers were basically second-class citizens in this school.

"Because," she began to say as she walked closer to me, "you were reading something else in my class." She took the book from my table and held it in the air for me and all the class to see. She had begun to irritate me, but I had to calm down and remain composed.

"I am sorry, Mrs. Qiu." I tried my best to feign remorse, but even a monkey would see through my weak ruse.

"Nice try," she replied.

"What is the square root of eighty-one?" she asked. I almost burst out laughing. Was this what she was making all the fuss about? She must have been dumber than I had thought.

"The answer is eleven plus seven minus thirteen plus twenty-four minus thirteen plus four minus eleven." I watched as the woman furrowed her brows trying to calculate the answer, probably to see if I was correct. I decided to help her out.

"It's nine," I answered after few seconds, the class filling with *oohs and aahs*.

Later that day, after school was over, I was called to the Headmaster's office. Upon entering, I saw my mother seated. I rolled my eyes, which made the Headmaster frown, but Mother remained unfazed, the same sad look in her eyes I always saw. The Headmaster made me write a formal apology to Mrs. Qiu. While writing it, I wondered if he ever got tired of making me write these. This was my fourth letter. I surmised he valued money over discipline, as my mother had probably bribed him.

Mother thanked him, and I left with her. We got in the car and went home. On the way, for some reason, I felt nervous. Mother and I had always been on good terms, but she was a woman of few words, which made it hard to communicate with her. I didn't feel the need to apologize because I didn't believe I did anything wrong, but I just wished she would say something. Anything.

"You do know your father will have to know about this, right?" she finally broke the ice.

"Yes, Mother," I replied quietly but audibly enough for her to hear. I knew what she meant. If she didn't tell him, one of the guards or even Li would inform him, and that would make him angry that neither Mother nor I had told him. Neither of us wanted to see Father when he was angry.

CHAPTER TWO

BEHIND CLOSED DOORS

When we got home, I kept wondering what Father would do this time. He had warned me if I had any further altercations or confrontations with a lecturer, he would have to have a talk with me. Maybe that was why I did it, to receive even a semblance of a scolding. Mother said he was coming back from Mongolia tomorrow, and that night I could not sleep.

"Stupid Mrs. Qiu," I said.

This was all her fault. If she had just let me do what I wanted and taken her humiliation like the lower citizen she was, this could all have been avoided. I got up from my bed and went down the stairs to try and relieve my stress by eating. At the kitchen, I saw my mother, hands on her head, sitting at the dining table with some water in a tumbler.

"Hello, Mother," I greeted her in my usual formal way. Everyone always said I tried too hard to act older than my age, but in all honesty, this was who I wanted to be: prim, collected and powerful like Father. Mother barely noticed and remained in her state. I could not tell if she had fallen asleep or was deep in her thoughts. I also could not see her eyes since they were covered by her hands, so I decided to take what I needed and go. I opened the refrigerator and scanned it. I took a milk carton and two dumplings before jamming the fridge shut. I turned around and saw Mother looking at me with her now-signature deadpan eyes. My shutting of the fridge must have woken her up or snapped her out of whatever trance she was in. Looking at Mother, I truly felt sad. Her sunken eyes mirrored how she probably felt inside, dark and devoid of life. I noticed that the crinkles at the side of each eye had become more prominent since the last time I had really taken a good look at them. Her messy hair fell haphazardly on her forehead, and her nose tilted slightly from the last time Father had broken her nose during one of his assaults. Ying Yue was a beautiful woman, but now she looked like a mess.

"Hello, Mother," I repeated myself, walking over to sit by her side. I had originally intended to go eat in my room but changed my mind after seeing my mother's state. She placed her arm around me, giving me a sheepish smile as she attempted to reassure me she was okay.

"Hello, dear," she said in her warm yet bold voice.

"You've been crying." Now being close to her, I noticed it. Her eyes were reddish. She immediately used her hand to wipe her face, sniffing a few times.

"I'm fine, dear," she assured me, giving me a tight hug.

"Is it because of me?" I asked. If it was, I would feel very bad. Mother had enough problems as it was.

"Oh no, Bat," she assured me, placing a palm on my cheek. "It's definitely not you. You are a blessing." She actually gave me a real smile this time, her crinkles becoming even more salient than they already were. I smiled back.

"Is it Father?" I inquired. Her smile slowly disappeared as her eyes wandered to the side.

"Don't worry about it, Bat," she replied. She then asked in a reprimanding tone, "So, how many times have I now been called to your school because of you?" It was obvious she was trying to change the subject. I wanted to point this out to her but realized talking about Father could be a sour topic for her, so I let it go.

"Four," I mumbled, looking down, expecting a scolding.

"Your father will not be happy," I heard her say and looked up. It seemed she was talking to herself, not me. This partly annoyed me.

"I'll try and cool him down before telling him," Mother assured me, rubbing my cheeks again. I always wondered why she did that since I had a lanky frame and apparently no cheeks whatsoever, but Mother always found some and said they were beautiful.

"The last thing we want is your father being in a bad mood when he finds out," she warned, and I knew what that meant. Father had never laid a hand on me, but that was always because I never gave him a reason to. I excelled in academics and always kept quiet and behaved when he had his friends or business associates over. The one issue I always had had always been with my lecturers, and even though Father didn't really seem to care initially, he eventually became annoyed due to the sheer volume of times he had to hear about it.

Mother and I talked and joked for a while that night. I thought to myself that this was the first time in a long while we had talked like this, and I appreciated every minute of it. Little did I know the next day was going to be the exact opposite.

Father arrived later than he usually did that day, at around six in the evening. I peeped through the window and saw him bang the door in annoyance, clutching his briefcase like he wanted to strangle the handle. My mother came to welcome him, but he barely replied to her greeting. He seemed to mumble something to her before briskly walking past her and into the building. She promptly followed with a worried look on her face. I began to get nervous. Initially, I wasn't too worried after talking with Mother, but now? I began fidgeting my fingers in anxiety. We lived in a big house, but I could still hear him shouting. I decided to stay in my room and feign sleeping.

A short while after, the door opened, and I knew Father had entered the room. Mother had probably told him, and he was upset. I closed my eyes and kept them shut, half-hoping that he would see I was asleep and not want to wake me up.

"I know you're awake, Bat," my mother mused, placing her hand on my shoulder. My eyes quickly shot open and I turned to look at her.

"We can't tell your father now," she said, a look of disappointment plastered on her face. "He just lost a huge contract because the client refused to agree to his suggestions." "We'll have to wait till he calms down. I'm sure—" She was cut off by the loud sounds of my father bellowing her name from the lobby. His voice reverberated throughout the house, and we both knew what that meant.

"Stay here. Act like you're asleep," Mother instructed, and I obeyed. She dashed out of the room, replying to my father's calls as loudly as she could. I remained silent and strained to try and hear what was going on, but I could only pick up on my father shouting without being able to make out what it was exactly he was saying. I decided to go down myself and see, my curiosity getting the best of me. I crept quietly out of my room and down the stairs, looking left and right like a thief about to steal. As I got closer to the source of the noise, I began to make out what my father was saying.

"I come back to find this?!" he exclaimed, evidently boiling with rage, from the sound of his voice. "While I am trying to secure a business deal that would put food on the plate for both of you, that brat is disrespecting my name in school and you are covering it up for him?!"

"I didn't—"

Something that sounded like a slap shut my mother up before she could finish her defense. The sound alone was enough to rattle me.

"Shut up! Why did I have to hear of the incident at the school from Li?! You had the chance to tell me, but you didn't!!" I finally understood what went wrong. Father had most likely asked Li for a status report on all the happenings in the house. Li must have overheard us talking in the car, and even though he didn't know what I did, even a simpleton would know I did something wrong for my mother being called to the Headmaster's office. Li couldn't lie to my father, no one could. They all feared and respected him too much to try something like lying. When Father found out, he probably confronted Mother about it and that led to this. I walked down and peeped until I saw him. He was livid. I could see my mother clutching her face and silently sobbing while he continued his rant, spewing out a litany of insults at her while she remained silent.

"Why didn't you tell me? I had a right to know!"

"I was going to but when you came back upset I didn't—"

Father hit her with another slap, making her scream and stagger backward. He moved closer and landed another slap which was likely harder than the preceding one, making me flinch in reflex. Mother shouldn't have mentioned that business deal, I thought. All she did was make Father angrier and remind him of not being able to close it.

"Are you talking back to me?!" Father asked, seemingly rhetorically. Whenever Father was angry, it was hard to tell if he wanted you to answer his questions or not. My heart sank seeing my mother curled up by the wall like a pet scared of its owner. Father looked down on her with a vicious scowl. I thought about going and stopping this. After all, it was I who caused this whole mess. I chose not to, my fear getting the best of me as I remained rooted to the spot, watching from afar. I always wondered how everyone in the compound was able to be quiet and let my father keep doing this over the years, even Ming. I then looked at myself and where I stood. Was I doing anything?

"Answer me! Do you now forget to respect your husband and talk back to him instead?!" he repeated the question.

"N-n-no, Chuluun," she managed to reply amid sobs. "I would never do that, I'm sorry."

Just then, I slipped from the stairs on which I landed on the ground with a thud. Father and Mother both turned around to my direction. Mother's eyes widened with a look of terror while Father's eyes glistened with anger. I just looked at them both, not sure what to do.

"You!" Father shouted, walking towards me. "Since you want to disobey me, I will teach you respect!"

"No!" my mother screamed as she ran ahead of him and stood between Father and me. I was shocked and so was he. This was the first time I had seen my mother stand up to my father in my life. My father's brows seemed to furrow even further.

"Please, just me," Mother said.

I watched as my father beat her into a stupor that evening. He broke her recently-healed nose, kept kicking her in the stomach while shouting profanities at her and even used a bat to hit her a few times. All I, Bat Erdene, could do was remain sprawled on the ground and watch as my father beat my mother because of me.

CHAPTER THREE

DEFLECTION

The beatings continued for my mother for two more years, and no one said or did anything. I tried to use school as an escape from what I had going on at home. I still had the occasional clash with lecturers, but nothing big enough to warrant my father's ire. Today, I was in school during break time when Yang ran over to me.

"Have you heard?" he asked animatedly.

"Heard what?" I retorted.

"There's a new student from America that just arrived today!" Yang said, the excitement evident in his eyes.

I was intrigued. The school had been boring to me for the past few years, but now at least an American student was a new level of intrigue that I had not expected. I wanted to go and welcome him, but I felt due to my standing in the school, it should be the other way around.

Classes finished that day, and I still didn't get to see the fabled student. I waited for a while, and yet Li had not arrived. I waited until I was the last person in front of the gate, or so I thought. Sitting down by the corner of the gate, I took out a dumpling from my bag and began unwrapping it to eat in an attempt to pass the time.

"Yo," I heard from behind, promptly turning to see who was still here by this time.

I saw a boy I had never seen before standing behind me. He was wearing the school uniform, so he had to be a student. He looked...there was a word for it. I knew I had read it somewhere...Caucasian! Yes, that was it. He had blonde hair, which I had never seen in person, and light blue eyes.

"I hear you're the one who runs this school, huh?" Even though I had already surmised this, his accent gave him away as the new American student.

"I guess you could say that."

"You have the best English I have heard since I arrived in China," he commended. "Someone would think you were British or American if they only heard you."

"I'll take that as a compliment, thanks."

"I'm Collins, by the way," he introduced himself, bending down and stretching forth his hand for a handshake, which I accepted. "Collins Stone."

I almost laughed at his surname. Stone? What kind of names do they give people over in the West? And this wasn't just his name; it was his family's name.

"I'm Bat...Erdene," I said while we shook hands.

"I know," he said with an ominous smile displayed across his face. "I think we're going to be good friends, Erdene."

I found his weird tone and demeanor unsettling.

"Uhh... I guess so." I was at a loss for words because I didn't know what to make of him.

Li then haphazardly drove into the drop-off. I turned around and wondered why because Li was a very meticulous driver, which was why my father liked him. My mother even always complained he was overly-cautious in his driving style.

"Get in, Mr. Bat," he said. I could see he was sweating from where I stood. He was also panting.

"Is everything okay, Li?"

"Please, Mr. Bat, could you just get in the car?" he implored in an aggressive tone that I did not take kindly to. "Please, I will explain everything."

I stood up, told Collins goodbye and hurriedly entered into the car with Li driving off hastily.

"What is it, Li?"

"It's your mother, Mr. Bat," he began to explain. "She is at the hospital."

Everything he said after that came as murmurs at me. My heart sank then began to bang as fast as possible. I started sweating profusely despite the air conditioner being turned on. I swallowed my saliva and tried to calm down. What happened? Was she alive? Where was Father?

"Mr. Bat... Mr. Bat!" Li snapped me back to reality.

"Your father is at the hospital. He told me to pick you up; we're going there now," Li explained.

"Is my mother alive?" I asked the question I had been dreading to ask since he informed me of her location.

"Everything's going to be okay, Mr. Bat," Li tried to assure me by deflecting the question.

"That is not an answer to my question," I sniped back at him.

"Mr. Bat, you need to calm down. W—"

"Calm down? Calm down?! How am I supposed to calm down when my useless driver comes late to pick me up then informs me my mother is at the hospital with no other helpful information about her condition?!" I cut him off.

"I know you are angry and scared, Mr. Bat," Li said calmly. "And I know you are trying to lash out at me as a way to express what you are feeling, but being angry at me will not help your mother. You need to be strong for her."

I wanted to insult him again but reconsidered and instead sat back in silence, my knees bouncing up and down in rhythm, unable to stay still. I hated admitting it, but he was right. I was deflecting. I didn't want to think about how bad things were with my mother at the hospital. Wait! What even put her in the hospital in the first place? How did I not lead with that?

"Li, what happened to Mother?" I asked sternly.

After a slight pause, Li replied by saying he did not know.

"What do you mean you do not know?!" I was about to go on another broadside at him.

"Your...father brought her out of the house, all bloody and beat up," he began to explain, "ordering me to take them to the hospital and saying that she was unconscious."

It was then it all clicked. I clenched my fists in anger, biting my lip until it drew blood. Li, looking up and seeing me via the front mirror of the car, further elaborated on the events following that. All the while he talked, I never said a word. I just listened carefully.

We reached the hospital about twelve minutes after we left the school. The moment the car stopped, I sprung out the door and sprinted into the hospital, Li chasing and calling after me.

"Good afternoon," I hoped the woman at the reception desk understood English since my Chinese was sketchy at best. "I'm looking for Ying Yue Erdene. She was admitted roughly thirty minutes ago."

She quickly checked the system prior to informing me of Mother's room number. By now, Li had caught up to me, and we both went up the stairs to her room. In the hallway, I could see my father coming out of the room. I tried running past him, but he held my hand with his.

"Your mother is resting now and will be back later this evening," he explained calmly. "Everything has been taken care of. She is fine."

"What happened to her?" I asked and was sure he could hear the anger laced in my voice.

"We'll talk about this at home," he said and tried to drag me with him, but I wouldn't budge.

"Why?! Because you know what you did?!" I raised my voice, much to his astonishment.

A couple of onlookers began taking notice of us, which was what I wanted. Father noticed and smiled at them until they turned their gazes back to their prior activities before he fixated at me.

"If you don't obey me right now and go home with me, I swear, you will regret it." He said it menacingly enough to instill some fear in me. The vein at the middle of his forehead had popped up, and I knew what that meant. I was not going to budge, however. Not until I saw Mother.

"I am not taking a single step with you until I see Mother," I spat back right at his face.

His eyes widened in disbelief, and a smile followed that, which unsettled me.

"Fine," he agreed, much to my surprise. "Let's go see her."

He dragged me with him to Mother's room. The moment I saw her, a mix of sadness and anger swelled up inside me, much greater than the anger I already had stored. I could see her black eye. She had a cut on her lower lip, forehead, nose, and cheekbone. Her nose seemed broken yet again, not to mention the numerous other bruises that were visible on her body. I was sure if I had time to hear from the doctors, she would have had even more internal injuries that were not visible to the naked eye. I tried running to her, but Father's grip was really strong, and he yanked me back. I looked up at him.

"Why?" was all I could muster. I could not fathom how or why a person could do this to another human being, let alone a man to his own wife. To my surprise, looking in his eyes, I saw remorse. His eyes were red, and he seemed confused like he also didn't know why he does this. I didn't care; he wasn't the victim here, she was.

"You WILL kill her, Father," I said quietly but sternly to him, tears now rushing down my eyes. "Please, please stop. I don't care how you want to do it, but stop."

I left him in front of the door and went back to the car with Li, who had kept his distance to give us some privacy. While at the car park, as I wiped the tears from my face, Li wrapped his arms around me and gave me a hug. It's like he knew I needed one. I broke down and cried into his chest. He just kept quiet and let me cry to my satisfaction.

We eventually got into the car and waited for Father. Li later received a call from Father instructing him to take me home without him. When I got home, I could see Ming was worried. The moment I got down from the car, I passed through the other guards and went to see Ming.

"Is she all right?" Ming asked, evidently worried about Mother's condition. He must have seen her when she was hauled out of here.

"Yes," I affirmed, looking down nervously. "She will be. She will be back later this evening."

Ming then brought me close and held me tight.

"I'm sorry, boy," he comforted me.

We talked a little while before I went to my room. I tried to read a book but gave up and flung it away. I couldn't concentrate.

Later that day, Father called for another driver to go pick him and Mother up. I waited for them at the porch until they arrived. Mother was brought out in crutches, and I immediately ran to hug her tight.

"Easy now," Father cautioned. "She is still pretty sore."

I thought to myself, 'Whose fault was that?'

We all went into the house with Loya, the maid who comes every day to clean the place and make meals before going back home, having already prepared a dish for the family. She welcomed us all and wished Mother well before leaving. Father went upstairs to change his clothes, but I stayed with Mother.

"Mother, why don't you leave him?" I suggested out of the blue. Even I was surprised I said that instead of using my inner voice. I looked at mother, and she seemed unsurprised I would say that. She must have thought about it a number of times.

"One doesn't escape a man like your father," Mother said, looking into the distance. "And besides, if I leave he will find someone new to take his anger out on. You."

My eyes widened as I finally understood. My mother might not have been the type to always hold my hand and tell me everything would be fine, but she was even more than that. She got beaten up frequently just for me. All her pain and suffering had been for me, and I couldn't even stand up for her when she needed me the most. What kind of a coward was I?

"Mother, what caused the fight this time?"

"Does it really matter?" she inquired. "Tomorrow it'll be another reason. Next week it will be something else. He doesn't really need a reason."

"Enough of this gloomy talk," Mother said, opening the covered plates to let the aroma of the meal filled the air. "Let's eat."

Father came out shortly after and ate in silence while Mother and I laughed and joked. After a while, he dropped his spoon and coughed audibly, his way of informing us he was about to say something he wanted us to hear.

"Ying Yue," he started, looking at her nervously. "I am sorry for all I have done to you."

I furrowed my brows and looked at him, I turned to Mother in shock and saw she was also astounded. She turned to me to see if she was the only one who heard what he had just said before we both turned back to look at Father.

"I really am, and I will try harder to control my anger," he said solemnly. "You might not believe this, but I do love you."

"I know, dear," Mother said with a smile.

Father simply nodded and left the dining room. Opening up and admitting he was wrong was incredibly hard for Father. In fact, in my entire life, this was the first time I have heard Father apologize. I smiled. Things were finally looking up.

Two days later, Father was at it again. It was like he had completely forgotten what he had said two days prior. He was upset that morning because his construction plans had been designed to the wrong specifications by the builders. See, Father was an architect. He had been moody all day, with no one able to cheer him up. At night, he and Mother were supposed to go out for dinner, but he asked her to change. When she had asked him why he slapped her.

An argument ensued, with Mother reminding him of what he had said days before. This only made him angrier and he began to beat her. I heard it all from the corridor and for the first time in my life, I went to my mother's defense. I pushed my father off her and, as a result, received the beating of my life. I smiled all through the beating Father gave me, as long as Mother was safe.

CHAPTER FOUR

TIPPING POINT

Collins and I had become really close friends. We seemed to be smarter than everyone around us, probably due to us being more exposed to other cultures. I had gone to America once when I was eight and he grew up there, plus our diction was much better than others. We were better than others. I began spending more time with him and less with my previous friends, which seemed to upset Yang, who was as clingy as a girl. Collins had even invited me over to his place, but I told him my father would kill me if he found out, which he would. Saying he would kill me wasn't too big of a stretch with the way he had been beating the living daylights out of me. I asked for it, though. Anytime I saw he was upset or sensed he was going to take it out on Mother, I would purposely annoy him or get in his way, causing him to beat me instead. Mother had told me to stop but I was having none of it. She had taken thirteen years of beatings for me, maybe even more. This was nothing.

I was in the restroom at school one fateful day, relieving myself, when someone entered the room. When I was done, I flushed and came out to wash my hands, only to meet Collins resting by the wall.

"Yo," he said in his signature greeting.

"Uhh...what are you doing here?" I inquired since he apparently had no intention of peeing.

"Straight to the point, I see," he chimed, moving closer to me. "I guess I will be, too."

Collins pushed me up against the wall. I was still confused as to what he was doing.

"Collins, what is the meaning of—"

He cut me off by kissing me on the lips. After a few seconds, I pushed him off me. Even though he was more built than me, I was taller than him.

"What is wrong with you?" I whispered. "Are you drunk?"

"Why didn't you push me back immediately?" Collins asked, a smirk plastered on his face. I was caught off-guard by such a question.

"I...I didn't understand what you were doing," I stammered.

"You didn't understand that I kissed you?" he asked with an eyebrow perked upward. "Have you never kissed anyone before?"

"Of course I have." It was the truth. I had been involved with girls before, but never with a guy.

"So, what's the problem? Because I know you liked it," Collins stated confidently and began moving closer to me again.

"Dude, seriously, stay back," I warned, but he just kept moving closer, slowly.

"I have watched you closely and spent time with you. You want this, you just don't know it yet," Collins mused as he placed his hands on my chest and pushed me against the wall again.

Why wasn't I running or pushing him away? Did I really like what he was doing to me? This was disgusting! How could two males be involved in sexual deeds like this? He kissed me again, forcing his tongue into my throat. Before I realized it, I was kissing him back.

"You see?" he said with a triumphant smirk, and I just stared at him in horror.

"No!" I screamed and pushed him away, running out of the restroom.

I avoided Collins throughout the rest of the day. When school was over, I impatiently waited for Li to come and pick me up. I had hoped he would arrive as quickly as possible so I wouldn't have to see Collins. Just then, I felt a hand grab my arm and I instinctively yanked my hand away. I swiftly whipped my head around and saw it was Yie.

"Sorry, I just wanted to see how you were doing," Yie said softly. "You've been spending more time with that American boy and less time with Yang and me, so I just wanted to see if we could have a time where all three of us could be together like before."

I remained silent and kept looking around. Yie scanned my face and noticed I was rattled.

"Is everything okay, Bat?" he asked cautiously, and I nodded a little too quickly.

I finally spotted Li as he stopped in front of me. I quickly hopped into the car without so much as a wave at Yie, and we drove off. On the ride home, I kept thinking what this meant. Was I broken? Did I need to be taken to a psychiatric ward or an exorcism? What annoyed me the most was that Collins was right, I did enjoy it. I didn't want to, but I did. I was still pondering on what this could mean when Li snapped me out of it.

"Are you okay? You look a little pale," he asked, a look of worry on his face.

"I'm fine. Do not worry about me, Li," I assured him.

He shrugged and kept driving.

When we reached home, I left the car and briskly walked into my house. I mumbled a greeting to Loya before walking up the stairs to my room. I kept thinking about what I was and what would happen if anyone knew. I looked out my window and saw Ming. I decided to go and ask him what to do. He knew all my secrets, what's one more?

"Hello, Ming," I greeted as I walked up to him.

He turned and smiled when he saw me.

"How are you, Bat?" he asked with a soothing smile. "I greeted you, but you didn't reply. You seemed deep in your thoughts."

I sat down on the pavement and he mirrored me.

"I...I had an issue at school," I started.

"What happened?" Ming asked, and I paused.

I didn't know how to tell him. Would he still see me as the same old Bat he cared about? He would chastise me, wouldn't he?

"Don't worry, I won't judge you," he said, placing his hand on mine. This made me more relaxed and I decided to tell him.

"I kissed a boy...or rather, a boy kissed me, and I liked it," I took off with my explanation. "I believe I might like boys." I couldn't look him in the eye. Silence filled the air.

"Do you not like girls?" I heard him ask. I could tell from his voice that he was slightly disappointed, but I also appreciated the fact that he didn't tell me that. Ming was an old-school man with old-school beliefs, but he never once attacked me for having beliefs or lifestyles that differed from his, and that was what I loved about him.

"I like girls, too," I replied nervously.

"I am not going to pretend that I am happy with what you said, but I do care about you, and it doesn't matter what you like. It matters who you are," Ming said while placing a hand on my shoulder.

This shocked me, and I finally had the courage to look at him. He was smiling. I hugged him tight, thanked him and proceeded to leave when he called me back.

"You should tell your mother," he advised.

"What? Of course not," I retorted. "I don't know how she would take it."

"That woman has done more for you than you can imagine. She loves you more than anything in the world. She won't reject you just because of this," Ming stated.

I told him I would think about it and left. I thought deeply about what he said for three days and surmised he was right. I summoned up the courage to tell my mother. She just placed her hands on her head after she found out I liked boys in a sexual way like I did girls. For several minutes, quiet filled the air. After a while, I decided to try and speak.

"Mother? I—"

"Your father must not hear this" were the only words that came out of her mouth.

CHAPTER FIVE

DAY TO REMEMBER, A NIGHT TO FORGET

After my talk with Mother, I found it very confusing to understand what it was exactly I did wrong. I wasn't sure, but I thought Mother couldn't just deal with any more issues from me that would make Father angry. Father had kept beating me on the regular and I kept taking it for Mother. This served as a form of release or distraction from the physical and emotional pain at home and I needed that. I really needed that. The other misdemeanors were one thing, this was a whole other. With tears rolling down her cheeks, she begged me vehemently not to tell my father or anyone, for that matter. Unbeknownst to her, I had already confided in Ming, but he surely was not going to tell Father. I told him about what Mother said and he told me even though he might not have agreed with the way she handled it, one thing was for sure: we could not let Father know. He went as far as saying that telling my father could signal my end and warned me sternly to not tell anyone. These reprimands only made my thirst grow and sooner rather than later, I had begun enacting my dark fantasies on my classmates by bribing them.

"Uhmm... I'm not sure about this, Bat," Ko said.

I ran my finger down his shoulder and moved closer to him. I could feel his breathing getting heavier.

"Why don't I double the yen?" I chimed.

Ko's eyes widened in disbelief. He quickly nodded before I began to kiss him, shoving my tongue inside his mouth. Ko groaned but I took it was a moan of pleasure. I was already aroused and hit him against the wall hard, which made him groan even harder. I began unbuckling my shorts as I went down his neck, trailing kisses on the way. Honestly, I didn't care if Ko liked it or not, I just knew I liked it, and that was all that mattered. When I finished pulling down my shorts, I commanded Ko to begin sucking my private member, which the terrified boy did. The amount of pleasure I felt was indescribable, even more, heightened by the fact that neither of us was supposed to be doing this. I looked left and right to see if anyone was around but saw nobody. We were at the back of the school, under a secluded shade, and it was during classes now, so I was fairly sure no one was coming there.

Closing my eyes, I savored every moment Ko did what I asked him to do. When I was done with Ko, I paid him the money and told him to leave, which the boy did. I waited a couple of minutes before going out myself so as not to arouse suspicion. When I entered his classroom, everyone's eyes turned to me, Mr. Oscar included.

"Bat," Mr. Oscar said in his refined English. He was one of the two only people better at speaking English than me, the other being Collins. He was also the only teacher I actually had time for or respected. "Where have you been all this while?"

"I had to go to the toilet, and it was a long one, sir," I replied while raising a brow and nodding to emphasize my point.

Mr. Oscar just smiled and waved for me to go sit down before continuing his class. As I sat down, I couldn't help but smile. The thrill was too exhilarating and only made me thirst for more. I wanted to do more and more, and "experiment" with the limits of my hunger. I had "used" four different boys now, all more than once, but that wasn't enough. I knew I needed to be careful, but I also had to take risks or the pleasure would be dulled.

Two years in and I had become a full-fledged bisexual. I had sexual relations with girls, but it was the boys whom I derived maximum joy and pleasure from. Maybe it was because it was frowned upon by society or the look in the boys' eyes when I threatened and forced them to do what I wanted. I had even made

Yang have sex with me with the aid of Collins, who was now my partner in crime. I had wanted him for a while due to his feminine look and mannerisms and had finally gotten him after he refused to take money. Collins pinned him down while I had my way with him. The more he struggled, screamed and begged, the more it aroused me, oddly enough. I knew no one would say anything. Who would dare? The shame alone they would receive was enough to dissuade them against trying anything of the sort. I had planned everything perfectly and most boys were afraid of me while the others respected me. Nothing could go wrong.

"Hello, Ming," I shouted from the car at Ming, who smiled and waved with one hand while he held open the gate with the other one.

His smile quickly dissipated when he noticed someone was inside the car with me. I calmly smiled and assured him that everything was fine. All this I did by shouting at him with the window wound down and the car moving into the car park. The car finally parked, and I came out with a friend.

"Ming, this is Chang," I began the introductions and gestured to Chang, who smiled and waved. "Chang, this is my second father, Ming." Ming shook the young boy's hand firmly.

"You are welcome to the Erdene residence, young man," Ming said with a warm smile.

After everyone had exchanged the necessary formalities, we both went inside with me leading Chang. On the way, I passed my mother, who just waved at us without a second thought. If only she knew what I had planned.

"Where's your father?" Chang asked, his legs dangling about in the air in a playful manner.

"Trust me when I tell you, you don't want to meet him."

"Is that so?" Chang said, now standing up.

I took time to truly view the accentuated features of my next prey. Chang had long, dark hair. Much longer than most boys I had seen. I told Chang I had invited him to supposedly aid him in an assignment. I had also *called on* Chang once before, but we only dabbled in the shallow things. Now that I had gone neck deep in it, I decided to try and penetrate every boy I had not been able to or was too scared to before.

I did what I wanted with him, threatening to kill him if he didn't cooperate. Honestly, I was never really going to do it, but he didn't know that.

This became a routine for me, bringing friends into my house to have sex with them under the pretense of having *guy time* or studying. Little did I know, my luck would soon run out.

On one fateful Friday, I was summoned to the Headmaster's Office. When I reached there, I saw Yang, my former friend, and his father. Yang's eyes were reddened, which made me come to the conclusion that he might have been crying.

"Mr. Erdene," the Headmaster began, trying to contain his delight, but I could see a smile creeping from the edge of his mouth. "We have been made aware of something gravely wrong that you have done."

"And what would that be, sir?" I retorted confidently, as if unfazed. I was truly scared now but they did not need to know that. The Headmaster just smiled at me, which further unsettled me.

"Did you rape this young man over here, Master Erdene?" he asked calmly.

I could clearly see Yang's father clenching the chair he was seated on as an attempt to control himself and not attack me. I looked at Yang in disbelief. This wasn't me feigning surprise to seem innocent, I was genuinely surprised that Yang had the guts to actually tell on me to his father and even the Headmaster.

"Answer the question, Master Erdene," the Headmaster prompted.

"No! I did not! What is this?! Are you joking?!" I denied all charges vehemently, shaking my head in disagreement. "How can you say something like this?! Just because we aren't friends anymore and I haven't found time for us to hang out together?!"

Yang was obviously too scared of me or broken by what I did to him to say anything to my face, which helped my case and made him look like he was lying. Yang began to cry with his father consoling him. The Headmaster just stared at me with disgust.

"So, I guess Ko Amin, Jin Choi, Rahman Abdul, Min Chen, and twelve other students have all been lying, right?"

I was stunned. How did they even know which students I had had sex with? Could it be?

"Collins Stone told us everything after we pressured him," the Headmaster stated. "He won't be expelled. He will be suspended because he gave you up and didn't really rape any of the students."

I was still flabbergasted. I swallowed my saliva and began to sweat. My view changed from looking at the Headmaster to Yang to his father then back to the Headmaster.

"You, on the other hand, will definitely be expelled," he said with a triumphant smile on his face. He always hated me due to my disregard for the teachers, himself and the rules at school.

"I...I d-d-di-didn't do an-any...anything." I stammered. That was all I could say.

"Why?" Yang managed to ask amid his sobs and sniffs. "Why did you ruin me?"

What was he talking about? He was the one who ruined me! If he had just kept his damn mouth shut, we all could have moved on with our lives.

"Oh, and we have contacted your father...directly," the Headmaster added.

This was when it really dawned on me how much trouble I was in. I began sweating profusely as I considered what Father would do to me when I got home. Do I run away from home? Maybe I can beg him, and he could forgive me. To make matters worse, Father was at home at the moment, not away on a business trip.

"I hope you get what is coming to you," Yang's father said, helping his boy stand up. "I really, truly pray you do." He turned to the Headmaster. "I'm sure you will see to it that he is expelled?"

"Trust me, I have been waiting for this day for a long time," the Headmaster replied with a smirk.

Yang and his father left the office.

"You can go," the Headmaster said dismissively, waving his hands for me to get out of his sight. "Your expulsion papers will be official soon."

Later that day, Li came to pick me up from school. When I entered the car, I could not believe who was already in there.

"Father..."

"Hello, Bat," he said, with an eerie smile. "I suddenly realized I had never followed you to school or picked you up from it."

We both knew this was a lie. He probably did not want Li to know what I had been up to, and honestly, neither did I.

"Father, I—"

"Not a word," he said.

I could see him clench his fists like he was trying his hardest not to hit me right then and there. Even though Father's mouth was closed, his jaw widened, which made me know he was clenching his teeth. We drove quietly to a few places where Father had some menial business tasks to attend to before finally arriving at the house at around 6:30 p.m. I saw Ming smile at me, but I was too preoccupied with what could be coming next for me to answer him in any way. We got out of the car and Father instructed me to go to my room, which I did. I saw Mother at the stairs waiting for me.

"Bat," she whispered. "What have you done? Why have you done this?"

I could see her eyes were filled with sadness, disappointment, and fear. She dragged me up, scolding me all through the way.

"I told you to quell these things, that your father would kill you if he found out. Why would you do this? Who knows what he will do to you now!"

She just kept on ranting. Technically, that was not what she said, but nevertheless, she had a right to be angry. Even though I never really considered how the other person I made have sex with me or engage in sexual relations with me was feeling, I had to know it was unfair to the person. Mother dragged me to my room and sat me down.

"Bat," she began, "you're only fifteen, and you are already doing this to boys? What do you do to girls, then?" She seemed to be half-hoping I would not answer for fear of what I might say.

"I don't do this kind of things to girls," I confessed. "It just feels better with boys. I don't know. I'm sorry, Mother."

She sighed in frustration. I was sure she was wondering how much more of this she could take. It was hard enough for her walking on eggshells around my father, but now she had to worry about my sexual tendencies? I felt a pang of guilt in me and sensed I had disappointed my mother.

"This is why I told you not to tell your father when you told me of your...condition."

I flinched a bit at her choice of words but knew this must be hard for her. She grew up in a society that condemns what I am.

"You knew?" Father said before entering the room. Mother pulled me behind her and faced him, her trembling hands holding mine viciously. We both could see he held his baseball bat in his hand, though now he used it more as a beating bat.

"I sent all the guards and maids away," Father said, the bat making an unsettling noise due to it being dragged across the floor. "I wanted to beat these devilish actions from you and I wanted no one to see what would be left of you. I don't want them knowing of this infection you have toward other boys."

My eyes widened in terror. He was crazy. Whenever rage clouded his judgment like this, he was immensely dangerous.

"But now, my wife knew all this time...and didn't tell me."

Father hoisted the bat at Mother, but I blocked it before attacking Father and pushing him against the wall. I wasn't the small, frail little kid he thought I was, but he was still stronger. He headbutted me before punching me in the nose. Blood gushed out as I staggered back and reached for my nose.

"Please, stop this!" Mother shouted, but Father, in this state, was basically blind and deaf to reason.

He bashed me in the head with his bat, which sent me to the ground almost instantly. I finally understood the term "seeing stars" as I began viewing strange sparkles while hearing my mother's voice faintly. She was by my side but looking at my father, most likely begging him to stop. I finally got full clarity at the same time he whipped her in the head with his bat. I jumped at him, causing the bat to leave his hand and fall to the corner of the room, and we both landed on the ground. Again, he overpowered me and punched me over and over and over again until Mother hit him over the head with a vase.

Father was shocked, and that only served to further his rage, if that was even possible. The vein bulged in his forehead. I could barely move, but I could definitely see. He walked over to Mother and held her neck, forcing her to the ground as he strangled her. I tried to move but my body wouldn't let me. Her eyes looked like they would pop out of their sockets as she tried in vain to peel off his hands. Seeing it was a futile effort and running out of air, she turned to me and stretched out her hands to me, as if asking for help. I tried to move and eventually succeeded, but all my hand could do was touch hers. I was too weak.

"F-Father...please," I struggled to say, but his eyes said he was already overcome with anger.

Slowly but surely, I saw the light at the back of my mother's eyes diminish and she died, eyes open, mouth open, looking at me.

For some reason, this was when my own rage kicked in. Something snapped in me and I felt a sudden surge of energy fueled by hatred, anger, and revenge. I yanked myself up, went for the bat, surged at Father and hit him across the head with it. He fell to the floor, but I did not relent. I hit him again and again and again until his brains spilled out of his broken skull.

I sat down in a pool of my father's blood and my parents' lifeless bodies.

CHAPTER SIX

AFTER ALL THESE YEARS

"Congratulations, Mr. Erdene. We look forward to working with Erdene Construction on this project," the man said over the phone.

I smiled, fist-pumping in the air and thanking him back before cutting off the phone. I then promptly called Ming through the window. He came out of his room to hear what I had to say.

"I got the deal!" I shouted from the top, and he grinned from ear to ear.

"Well, then come on down so we can celebrate!" he said. "I have a nice bottle I have been saving for a good occasion."

I quickly rushed down past the guards and maids, sprinting through them with reckless abandon in order to get to Ming. By the time I got to him, he had already gone into his room and come back with two glasses and a nice bottle of champagne.

"I pay you too much," I joked with reference to how costly the wine looked as Ming poured it into the tumblers.

"I'm worth it," he replied with a smile, and we both laughed.

Ming had been with me for the past eleven years, ever since my father died and I took over the company. After what I did to Father, I was put on trial, but it wasn't really hard to prove my innocence even though I was not. Since Father had sent all the guards away, only Ming was around because he lived in the compound. After killing Father, I ran to Ming for help and explained all that happened to him. He told me to say it was self-defense and that Father had been beating both Mother and me for years. He was sure all the staff would back me up because everyone had known what Father had been doing, but nobody had

had the courage to step up against him. Since no one was around, Ming was willing to perjure himself in court to protect me and my future. Everything went as planned, and numerous employees, including Li, stepped forth in court to testify on how much of a bad man Chuluun Erdene was at home, as opposed to the symbol of power and elegance he portrayed to the people of Chengdu and, by extension, the world.

I had always been close to Ming, but since that day, I swore I would keep repaying him for giving me a chance at life for the rest of my days. I bumped up his salary to more than three times what he had originally gotten and even asked him to come with me when I was finally moving to Bangkok, a request he gladly accepted.

I still continued having sex with boys...young boys. Now that Father wasn't around, I could do what I want, and everything that bastard owned was now mine. At first, running the business was not easy. Even though I had no prior experience in architecture or construction,

I had read a whole lot about the subject in anticipation for the day I might have been able to work under Father and help him in the day-to-day activities of the company. Funny how that worked out.

Even though I knew the theoretical aspect of the books and the balancing of sheets, I still needed people with the practical know-how of how to construct the buildings and other infrastructures. I eventually hired people to work under me and handle all that while I focused on the money and business side of things.

"Tomorrow, it'll be eleven years," I said to Ming, reminiscing about my mother and all she suffered.

"Yes, I know," Ming said, to my surprise. I didn't think he thought about that night as much as I did.

"You think you're the only one who has regrets?" he said after noting my surprise. "I do, too. Your mother endured a lot."

I looked at the ground in shame. I could not help her, I was useless. She needed my help more than once, and I hid. Even when she needed me the most I was still weak.

"I don't think..." I started to say while looking up at the sky. "I can remember a time when I saw her truly happy."

"I can," Ming quickly said, which made me whip my head over to him. "I can recall many times when I saw true happiness in her eyes."

"You know what all those things had in common?" he asked, and I shook my head. "You."

He smiled before taking another sip from his glass of wine. I smiled as well and did the same.

"Although, I will say, your mother would be disappointed in your other activities," Ming chimed calmly.

I frowned and glared at him.

"What's that supposed to mean?"

"You know what I mean." Ming's tone quickly became serious. "I can try and understand you wanting to do whatever you do with both men and women, but why do they have to be kids and young boys?" "It's not right."

This annoyed me. Who was he to tell me what was right and wrong? I decided not to push the matter. Instead, we both drank in silence.

A few months later, I was in downtown Bangkok, a commercial area of the city with more people than one can count. I was unveiling one of the buildings constructed by Erdene Construction as per the request of the owner. After I cut the ribbon and the formalities were over with and the reception had begun, I noticed a beautiful woman standing in the corner. Pitch-black hair at shoulder length, falling over dark brown eyes. Her pointy nose and full, luscious lips were a rarity among Asians.

"Hello, dear," I said in my usual charming way as I reached where she stood.

"Hi," she responded with a quick smile.

"I saw you from the other side of the room and came to the conclusion that I had to talk to you," I said. "My name is Bat Erdene, I'm the—"

"The one in charge of the construction contract on this building," she finished, much to my surprise.

"I am a reporter for the Bangkok Paper," she explained, and I nodded.

"So, Reporter..."

"Ting-Wei."

"That's a beautiful name."

"Thank you."

"So, Reporter Ting-Wei, do you have any questions for me on the specifics of this building?" I asked. I had hoped to use this as a route to engaging in an enthralling discourse with her.

"Sure, Mr. Erdene," she replied and grinned.

"Please," I interjected, holding her hand with mine, "call me Bat."

That was the first discussion of many, for the woman eventually became my wife.

CHAPTER SEVEN

OLD HABITS DIE HARD

"Shut the fuck up, you little shit!" I commanded as I swiped the young boy another slap across the face.

The helpless child held his cheeks and retreated to the corner of the room, folding himself like a ball. As I glided over to my prey, the fear in the boy's eyes and the position he was in suddenly became so familiar.

"Mother?" I asked in confusion, and the assailed mirrored my look of confusion, only that he was laced with fear.

Then it hit me, why I was remembering Mother at this time. I quickly recalled my mother crawling to the corners and edges of the wall and curling up into a ball to try and defend herself against Father's attacks. Placing my hands on my head, I staggered until I landed on the bed. The boy was still rattled, clutching the reddish cheeks of his fear-filled face with his palm.

"Get out," I growled, and the boy quickly put on his clothes and ran out of the hotel room.

The guards were outside, so they would get him. I stared at the ground for a while after the boy had left. What was wrong with me? What would my mother say about all this? She wasn't too fond of the idea that I was as attracted to men as I was to women in the first place, so how would she react if she found out I was taking advantage of homeless boys and bringing them to a hotel room to rape and enact other dark fantasies on them? I began to cry. I didn't even realize when the tears started rolling down my cheeks. Tears poured endlessly as I gnashed my teeth, falling into the rug in drops. I had caused Mother so many problems while she was alive. The beatings, the fact that she stayed with Father, and her death. All because of me. Now I was still causing her to be sad even in death? What kind of a devil child was I?

I put on my clothes, took my belongings and left the hotel. As I walked to my car, I kept on thinking about Mother. This was the first time I had seen her or felt that way when I was with a boy, and I didn't like it. However, these were also my sexual urges, and I couldn't just turn them off. I had to act on them.

I had been married to my dear Ting-Wei for over two years now, and things were looking rosy. Hopefully, we could add a third member to our small family, but I could be a good and loving husband while enjoying myself in hotels like these. What Ting-Wei didn't know wouldn't hurt her.

I came out of the hotel with my head down, covertly looking left and right with the hopes that no one would see me. I briskly got into my car and drove off. When I got home, I saw Ming opening the gate and waved at him. He did not wave back but opted to open the gate quietly while I passed through. I knew he was not happy, and I knew why. I drove into the compound and parked my car.

"Ming," I beckoned as he locked the gate in silence. "Is everything all right?"

Ming just looked at me with a blank expression.

"No, sir," he said bluntly and began to walk back to his room.

"Hey, hey, calm down."

I rushed after him and held his hand as I tried to get him to tell me what was wrong. I had my own beliefs on why he was angry, but I wanted to hear him say it. Ming sighed and turned around to face me.

"Sir, I have known you all your life," he began and I nodded affirmatively, "and I have seen how you and your dear, late mother suffered at the hands of your father and his terrible behaviors."

"Where are you going with this, Ming?" I asked sternly.

"I am saying after seeing how much your father was a bad husband to your mother, you decide to do the same to this nice woman over here?" Ming explained. "It was one thing when you weren't married. I still didn't like you raping young, innocent boys, but this? When you are married? You have gone too far, Bat."

I knew this was it. Before he even finished, I was already boiling in anger. How dare this common gatekeeper talk to me like this and have the guts to compare me to the bastard of a man that almost ruined my life?

"Let me get one thing straight with you," I said boldly to Ming's face. I was taller than him, which made me move closer to him, so he would look up. "You are a gatekeeper. I am your boss. You have no say in how I live my life or should live my life." Ming just looked at me with sadness and pity, which made me even angrier.

"I am just trying to help you, Mr. Bat," Ming softly stated, placing a hand on my shoulder. "You are lost, and you need to find yourself. Let me help you. I see you as my own son."

Ming had lost his child and wife when he was much younger, which was probably why he had taken such a liking to me when I was young. He had always told me I looked like his son, but that did not excuse the way he was behaving. When I was younger, Father kept laying all the rules on what I could and couldn't do. I did not need another father giving me more stupid rules.

I don't care what you want, I told him while slapping his hand from my shoulder to his utmost surprise. You are not my father, and I am not your son. My father is dead, as is your son".

"I think we have been too close that you have forgotten your station. From now on, we will have a simple working relationship. I tell you what to do, you nod and say *yes sir* and go do it," I started with my soliloquy as Ming just looked at me, stunned at the words protruding out of my mouth. "And if I ever hear even a single complaint about this issue from your ungrateful mouth, I will fire you.

"And remember you were an accomplice to what happened that night," I whispered to him. "If anyone found out, you would be going to jail because you have no one within the police in either Chengdu or Bangkok who would help you. I do. I will get away with it, but I promise you, you won't. So, any smart plans you might have had about telling my wife, it is I like to do, zip it and do your damn job."

"Yes, sir. As you wish," Ming said and turned around to leave.

"Did I say you could leave?" I wanted to humiliate him even more. He needed to get the message that no one should think they are on the same level as me. He needed to *obey my authority*.

"No, sir," Ming replied, turning back to look at me.

An awkward moment of silence ensued where we both stared at each other.

"You can go," I said and waved him dismissively. I turned around as I saw a few guards looking at us from afar.

"What the hell are you all looking at?!" I shouted at them. "Get the hell back to work!"

They all walked around briskly like they actually had stuff to do at that moment. Meanwhile, I stormed into my house. Seeing Ting in the kitchen, I went over to her and gave her a long, passionate kiss.

"What was that for?" she asked with a smile, clearly surprised at my random display of passion.

"Nothing, just a man kissing his lovely wife," I replied, making her grin and kissing me again.

Later that evening, as we both ate in the dining area, Ting decided to bring up the elephant in the room.

"So," she dropped her spoon, which made me know to drop mine and listen to her. I thought she was going to tell me about her day or someone she had an issue with so I could support her. "What happened between you and Ming?"

I rolled my eyes. I couldn't believe that was what she was asking about.

"Don't worry about it, dear," I assured her, but she frowned. Being a journalist, Ting was a very inquisitive person and got frustrated when she wasn't given a straight answer. "Ming and I just got into a difference of opinion. We have known each other for a long while and that makes him not know his place sometimes. I simply had to remind him." I explained as best I could without letting her in on the details.

"Well, whatever it is, I hope you both sort it out," she said before continuing with her food. She seemed satisfied with my answer.

The next day, I went to another hotel after having my contacts find and bring another homeless boy to me. As I entered, I saw a light-skinned boy with brown hair and eyes. I was completely enamored by him.

"Leave us," I commanded, and the guards quickly dissipated.

I took a few seconds to take another look at the scared little boy. He looked no more than twelve, which only made me want him more. I moved closer to him slowly, step by step. With each step I took, he flinched and reacted by moving backward, making me feel like I had power over him.

"What is your name?" I asked in an authoritative tone while still walking closer to him.

He didn't reply, shivering just at the sound of my voice. This annoyed me. I wanted him to obey. He must obey me. I would teach him to comply.

"Fucking answer me!" I barked at the prey, and it whimpered at the loudness of my voice. "You don't want to see what I would do to you if you don't answer."

I had asked them to find victims who could speak and understand basic English or at least just understand. I wanted them to hear me when I talked and obey me instantly. That was the whole point of all this, control. To have someone to do what I wanted when I wanted it with no complaints or arguments.

"Hakim," he replied softly.

I had reached him by now and placed my hand on his cheek. His face felt rough, probably due to the hard life he might have had before being brought here. I pulled him close to me and hugged him warmly. It was all part of my ritual, butter them up before the real thing begins.

"Hello, Hakim," I said, still holding him tight. "I am Bat. Don't worry, I will not hurt you," I assured him before letting him go. I looked at his face and saw he was still unconvinced.

'Smart boy,' I thought to myself.

"Stand up," I ordered.

He was taking too long to move due to still being afraid and I snapped, slapping him across the face. The slap I gave him was so hard it made him fall from the bed and unto the ground.

"I said stand up, you animal! Obey!" I hollered.

The boy quickly stood up, his eyes now red.

"Oh, you want to cry?" I asked sarcastically. "The time for you to cry is still coming, trust me."

His eyes widened in fear of what was to come.

"Take off your clothes."

He quickly did so, fearing another slap from me. This gave me great pleasure, having someone to order around as much as I wanted. When he was fully naked, I took my time looking at him and scanning his features. He was not as skinny as the other homeless boys before him, having a little meat on his torso and limbs. All in all, he had very smooth skin considering what he possibly could have gone through as a person without a home.

"Turn around," I said, and he did as he was told.

I ran my thumb and index finger through my chin as I looked at his small buttocks. I stood up and walked over to him, holding his neck from behind. I dragged him with me to the bathroom where I told him to have his bath. Hakim cried as he washed in front of me in the bathroom, but I was completely oblivious to his pain due to being aroused. I slapped him when his sobs had become too annoying for me to keep listening to.

"Shut up and wash!" I screamed, and he quickly limited the audibility of his sobs.

When he was done, I gave him a towel to get dried and dragged him by the hair to the bedroom. I slapped him again and told him to shut up, humping at the helpless boy until I was finished. I had sex with him two more times before calling for the men to come and take him out of my sight.

After they had done this, I sat alone by the side of the bed, feeling remorseful. It was always like this, and yet I just could not stop.

CHAPTER EIGHT

SUSPICIONS

I t had been four years into mine and Ting-Wei's marriage now but we were still yet to have a child. I was not worried, however, because I did love my wife and didn't marry her to be a breeder of children. I married her because I loved her. I was not really a religious person, but she was. She was a Catholic, which was quite rare in Bangkok. She made me pray with her that we would expand our family beyond just the two of us.

I came back from "work" one day, which was another way of saying I went to a hotel and slept with a young boy, and heard the music. I knew Ting-Wei loved music, but this was a bit too loud, wasn't it? I followed the sound up the stairs to its origin and met Ting standing by the king-sized bed in our room. She had her back towards me and was swaying and dancing.

Due to the volume of the song, she had not even heard me drive up, enter the house or walk up the stairs to where she was. I walked over to the stereo and paused the music, causing her to turn around in surprise to see who it was that had done it. The moment she saw me, her eyes lit up and she ran to me, jumping on and hugging me. I wrapped my arms around her waist, holding her in place. We remained that way for a few seconds before I put her down.

"What's the cause of the celebration?" I inquired, smiling only because she was, and I assumed there was good news.

"I went to see the doctor today," she said, and I quickly grew concerned, "because I missed my period."

I gave her a "are you serious" look and she nodded, grinning from ear to ear.

"I'm pregnant!" she screamed before we embraced each other in a hug again.

I couldn't believe it! I was going to be a father, a much better one than my own father. I had always wanted a full family of my own, and now it was going to be a reality. I hugged Ting tight and before I knew it, I began to cry.

"What's wrong?" she asked, clearly concerned by my change in mood. "Are you not happy?"

"I am...I am," I assured her, wiping away my tears. "I just wish my mother was here to see this."

I had told her little about my family. Since both my parents were dead, I felt no need to rehash the past. She kept inquiring until I finally told her about my mother, though not everything. I refused to talk about my father.

"I'm sure she would be happy and proud of you, Bat," Ting comforted me, dragging me to the bed and placing my head on her thighs. She was a very caring person, but that was not all I loved about Ting. She was also feisty and passionate, never backing down, which was what made her a good reporter.

We announced to all the staff that we were expecting a baby and were congratulated accordingly. We even threw a small party for just us and the staff to celebrate the good news. At the party, I could see every staff member I had on my payroll except one, Ming. I went outside the house to his room and knocked on his door. No reply. I knocked again, and Ming opened the door after unbolting the lock from the inside.

"What can I help you with, sir?" he asked curtly.

"Ming, there is a party. Come and have some fun," I urged, gesturing to the building. "You congratulated Ting and me this morning, didn't you? Aren't you happy for us?"

"I am, sir," Ming answered with a bored look in his eyes. "I would rather not come to the party, sir, unless that is an order," he said, referring to the day I embarrassed him and said he had to obey my every order.

I knew I went overboard that day. I was angry and hated the fact that he compared me to my father, which was why I had acted that way, and my pride would not let me go to him to apologize.

"Ming," I called while looking at him. "I'm sorry, okay? I was angry. You said I was like my father and that just ticked me off. I'm sorry I lashed out at you." I tried to make my case, not even sure if he understood some of the words I used.

"You don't need to apologize to me, sir," Ming stated like a robot. "I will always be loyal to you despite your threats and lifestyle. That I swear." He was sincere this time and I could see it in his eyes, which made me feel all the more guilty for threatening him with jail time. "But if I am not obligated to come for the party, I would rather not go."

I nodded. "You are not, Ming."

"Okay, sir. Thank you for the invite and good night," he said and closed the door on me.

Nine months later, Ting-Wei and I welcomed a bouncing baby girl, who we named Shu-Chen. Even after a baby girl came into our lives, and I had a loving wife and a good business, I still continued to dabble in the dark arts of pedophilia. I had even begun to do it when I traveled to Chengdu, Beijing, Mongolia, and Zhengzhou. I kept this up without thinking of all that I had. I became so addicted to the rape of young boys that I stopped touching Ting in bed, which she noticed, and began staying much longer than necessary on trips, completely neglecting her. After it had gone on for a while, she decided to confront me about it.

I came back from a four-week trip to Zhengzhou—I had been getting more contracts there recently—and Ting prepared a lavish meal for me without the aid of the maids. She wanted to do it all herself.

"Wow" was all I could say as I stared at the food before me. "You really went all out, didn't you?"

"Since you haven't been home in a while, I wanted to treat you to a traditional wife cooking to show you how much I have missed you," she explained.

I gave her a kiss prior to chomping on the food. After I was done, we cuddled on the bed while we talked.

"My story was published on the front page last week," she mused.

I looked at her in pride and kissed her on the forehead.

"Well done, dear," I praised.

She then moved closer to me and I knew what she wanted. She gave me a long, passionate kiss, her tongue and mine in unison. She began unbuttoning my shirt, but I stopped her.

"Dear, I'm a little tired from the trip," I explained. "I think I just need some rest tonight."

She frowned at me and moved back.

"Nice lie," she said to my surprise. "So, how long have you been cheating on me?"

"What?!" I exclaimed.

I was truly shocked that she was asking such a question. How could she have even known? Did Ming tell her? No, that's not possible. Ming would never betray me, regardless of him not agreeing with my actions.

"What's her name? Do I know her?" She kept on asking a new question before I even had time to process the last one. The fact that Ting said 'she' made me realize that she was just acting like a worried wife, thinking her husband was cheating on her because he had refused to have sex for a few months now. This wasn't wrong, either, because I was cheating on her, just not with women.

"What are you even talking about?" I feigned ignorance, making her annoyed.

"Today it is you are tired, last month it was you had a stomach ache, and the other day it was you had work. Do I look stupid, Bat?" she snarled. "You have to be cheating on me or else why would you keep refusing to have sex with your own wife?"

She made a compelling argument, but I had to convince her this was not the case.

"Ting, I swear to you, this is not what you think," I said calmly. This seemed to make her cool down a bit. I knew I needed to say more.

"I'm sorry I have not been active sexually, but you have to understand, work has been draining me both emotionally and physically. I had not even noticed it had gotten to the stage where you and I had not had sex for this long. I promise you, I have never and I would never cheat on you. You are my love and my all. Please, trust and believe me. I'm sure you noticed I have been having longer trips than before. The work is a little overbearing and that's why I have been so distant. It doesn't mean I don't still find you attractive or no longer love you," I lied eloquently in my monologue, and by the time I was done, I could see she was clearly convinced.

"I believe you," Ting said with a smile. "I love you, Bat Erdene."

"I love you, too, Ting-Wei Erdene," I replied.

She kissed me, and we made love that night. After that, I never forgot to have sex with my wife, so I could throw her off my scent. I still loved her, but I loved my other thing, too.

CHAPTER NINE

NAIL IN THE COFFIN

"Get him out of my sight," I ordered, and my men complied, taking the young child from the bed and away from the hotel room.

I sat down, thinking about my wife, Ting-Wei, my daughter, Shu-Chen, and, of course, Mother. The females in my life had always made me strive to be a better man and caring person, not this. I needed to do better, be better. I couldn't keep indulging in these kinds of things, no matter how much dark pleasure I gained from them. If I continued down this path, I really would become like Father, and that would be the worst possible thing that could happen to me. I pondered on the life I had led for at least thirty minutes before getting up, ready to leave. I knew all I had thought about and resolved would go down the drain the moment I had my urges again. I was conflicted but did not know what to do. I had become a prisoner of my perversions.

I got into my car as discretely as possible before being driven off to work. Work had become strenuous and hard these days. We had been getting fewer and fewer offers due to the rise of other architectural firms who offered to do the same work for less as a means to boost their brand. We were still one of the top construction companies in East Asia, but I was not happy with the recent decline in fortune, no matter how slight it may be.

When we got to the office, I got in and went straight for the elevator with several people greeting me on the way. I ignored them all. I needed to redirect my disappointment in myself at someone else. I was supposed to meet with the architects and engineers responsible for the construction aspect of my business to discuss how we could improve our profits. We had hoped that by bringing our heads together, we could find a viable solution for our menial problem. Despite it being a minute problem at the moment, it could have far-reaching consequences. I got into the Conference Room, where I could see all of them already seated, leaving my bodyguards at the door to stand watch.

"Welcome, Mr. Erdene. We w—"

"I don't care what you were saying before I came," I began my tirade. "I care what you do. You all better have a good reason why our profits are down." My voice was calm, but a growl of anger lurked beneath it. I knew it wasn't their fault. I did not care.

One of the men decided to be their spokesperson as he addressed me.

"Mr. Erdene," he began in an authoritative tone which I did not take kindly to, "we have done all you asked. We handled the construction of all the buildings efficiently and have had no unforeseen incidents or collapses in all the years we have worked for you. If the profits are reducing, don't you think that is a problem originating from the business side of the company, not the construction aspect?" he explained eloquently. Mr. Cass was American, after all.

"You are fired," I said bluntly, much to the surprise of the five men in the room.

Mr. Cass thought I was joking at first, chuckling at the thought of it. By the time I had signaled to my guards to have him escorted out of the building, it had dawned on him that his time was up. The other four just looked on, astounded at what had just happened.

"You can't do this!" was all he kept shouting. I didn't care. Authority had to be obeyed, like Fath...never mind.

I turned and looked at the rest of the men.

"Anyone else wants to air their opinion on how I run my business?" I asked calmly, spreading my hands to the side as a gesture urging them to speak.

They all just looked on, frightened.

I left them to handle it, even though we should have done it together since they knew nothing of the business and account aspects of the company. Leaving work early and having already had my fill of young boys, I suddenly found myself free for the day. I didn't want to go home because the guilt of my actions had weighed on me recently. Every time I held my daughter in my arms, with every kiss I laid upon my wife, I felt this pang of guilt in my soul. I had given up on stopping, though. It had gone on for too long, and the *sessions* had become as much a part of me as breathing had. It was almost like a drug. Scratch that, it was a drug.

"Sir?" I was snapped away from my thoughts and back to the car by my driver.

"Are you all right, sir?" he asked. I could see through the rear view mirror that he looked genuinely concerned for my well being.

"Yes, I'm fine," I replied, sitting up before relaxing in the seat.

"Where would you like to go next, sir?"

"Take me...to the Catholic Church."

I knew he didn't need to specify where the church was because my driver, Cheng-Han, was a Catholic. I had never been a religious person. Both Father and Mother had been Buddhists; Mother more so than Father, but neither of them was really deep in their religious beliefs, Father because he was consumed with work and Mother because she did not want to defy father. This made me indifferent about not only Buddhism but religion in general. When I married Ting, I started becoming sparingly involved in Catholicism but never really committed and went all in like she did. We even had Shu-Chen baptized in a Catholic Church at Ting's request.

We finally arrived at the church, Saint Margaret's Catholic Church. I got out and told Cheng to wait in the car before proceeding into the building. I got in and saw only three people sitting in the pews, seemingly praying or meditating. I sat down in the back and let my mind wander to my past. I remembered Mother's death and how it was my fault. I had caused the whole scenario that led her to keep the secret from Father. If I had not acquired these terrible urges, none of this would have happened. I would have had Mother, alive and well, but I would have also had Father alive. Maybe he would have killed us both by now if I hadn't killed him. I had been better since then, at least I thought I was. Everything seemed to be going great except for the uncontrollable arousal I got around young, helpless boys.

I looked up and saw the confession box. I walked there regally in silence, joining my hands together as a show of piety and humility. I entered the box and could see the silhouette of another human on the other side. I coughed once before beginning.

"Bless me father, for I have sinned. This is my first confession of the year," I stated calmly as the priest listened. "I have lied, cheated, fought and even killed. I always thought that would be the worst of my sins, but it's not."

"What would you term worse than the taking of a life?" the man at the other side of the room asked calmly.

I took a moment to pause, wondering how I would say it without seeming like a broken person.

"I...I just don't want to disappoint those I care about. My wife, my daughter. I keep making the same mistake over and over again," I replied cautiously.

"And you fear this sin worse than murder will hinder you from that," the priest surmised, and I affirmed. "Why don't you stop it, then? I know that is easier said than done, but if you truly value your family and do not want to lose everything, I would suggest you desist from this act."

"What if I can't stop?" I asked, the defeat evident in my voice.

"My child, that is why you need God," the priest advised. "Pray. Ask for guidance. Something like this could lead you down a path you cannot return from."

"You have made it this far despite your trespasses, and there is still hope for you now, son. Whenever you decide to commit this *sin*, remember what you have now, what you could lose, and pray. Never forget to pray," he warned as nicely as possible.

I left the church surprisingly optimistic. I had decided not to remain a prisoner of my urges and would finally be turning over a new leaf. Not only for Ting and Shu but for myself. What I was doing to these innocent boys was wrong, regardless of how much pleasure I derived from it. From now on, it had to stop. I was truly becoming my father as Ming had alluded to. I was at the edge, and if I continued down this road, just one more hit could send me tumbling over and into the abyss. These were just some of the things my mind ruminated on as Cheng drove me home. The father had given me a penance, and to my surprise, I was going to do it. I brushed my thumb and index finger against the rosary I bought just outside the Chapel.

I got home and saw Ming at the gate. He opened it quietly and bowed his head in my direction when the car went past him into the compound. Even though he had been the epitome of a hard worker, his relationship with me had been distant and strange since the day we had our incident. This made me sad, especially since I knew he was not wrong, and all that he said that day came from a place of love and affection. I came out of the car and waved to Ming, who waved back with a smile, before retreating to his favored plastic chair. He loved it so much he brought it with him from Chengdu, yet it was surprising it had lasted this long. I walked into my home feeling refreshed and happy to be there for the first time in a while. Ting had been acting weird for a week now, so I was planning on talking to her about it rather than ignoring her like I had been doing for the past few days. It had been a year since she confronted me about cheating on her. She asked me about it again a month ago, saying her friends saw me coming out of a hotel. As expected, I denied it, but she was smart. I had to stop before she found out by herself.

"Tiiing! I'm hoooome!" I sang as I walked past the living room to the kitchen to see if she was there. She wasn't. I walked up the stairs, still calling her name but got no reply. I finally found her in our bedroom, sitting on the chair at the edge of the room, facing me with a large brown envelope in hand.

"Hello, dear, I wanted to talk to you about something important," I said as I walked towards her. Even though I was smiling, she gave me a cold stare. "I noticed you have been acting upset or angry recently and wanted us to talk about it. I'm sorry I didn't ask you about it sooner, but I am willing to now." I explicated how I felt as best I could to her. I squatted so I could be at her level since she was seated and placed my palm on her knee.

"What is wrong?" I asked softly.

"Look me in the eye," she requested, sitting up and facing me straight on, "and tell me you are not cheating on me."

My eyes widened. Did she know? Was that what was in the envelope? Even though I was panicking, I knew I had to show a facade of calm. That was probably a ruse to get me to confess, and there was nothing in the envelope. I could just tell her the truth and beg for her forgiveness, maybe that was why she was asking me one more time. Yes, I decided I would do that.

"No," I replied. "I am not." What was wrong with me? "I swear to you, dear." Why was I saying this? "I have never and will never cheat on you." I lied straight to the face of the woman I loved. I was a coward...again. Mother would roll in her grave.

A tear escaped Ting's eye, strolling down her cheek and jawline before falling to the ground. She handed me the dreaded envelope, and I hesitated to open it. Did she really have proof I was cheating on her?

"Open it," she urged, and I looked up at her expressionless face. "You're telling the truth, right? You haven't cheated on me."

I reluctantly opened the envelope and shoved my hand in, bringing out a set of pictures of me entering several hotels and boys being dragged out of them. I knew this wasn't enough to make her conclude I was cheating on her with little boys.

"So?" I asked, and she scoffed, still partly surprised I was denying it.

"I went to every one of those hotels and bribed the receptionists there to find out what you were doing there," she said while staring at me, her blank expression still conspicuous, "until I found the time you paid with your credit card. I then found the receptionist on duty that day in every one of them and even talked with the attendants that brought room service. They all said the same thing. You had your guards bring a young boy to your room. At least three attendants involved in room service said you had sex with those boys, the rest weren't able to give any relevant information because your guards always offered to take it in. Some insisted, however, and went in."

By the end of her soliloquy, I was already sweating like a rabid dog. Was she that determined to find out what I had been up to? How did she even get these pictures in the first place?

"That wasn't enough for me," she continued, completely unfazed by my reaction. "So, I was able to bribe one of the guards that followed you to tell me the truth. He did."

I wanted to get angry and ask who the guard was, but I knew I was the one in the hot seat now. She was a journalist, and I should have known her bravery and curiosity would overcome her fears or trust.

"T-Ting, dear, I... I-I can explain," I said, finally admitting it yet still trying to salvage the situation. Her eyes flared up in anger the moment I said that, and she stood up and turned her back to me.

"While I was feeding, bathing and taking care of our fifteen-month-old daughter, you were raping young boys," she said it as if she couldn't believe it herself.

I didn't even know what to say that could make her feel better. I couldn't explain it myself. I had to say something to ease her pain.

"It's bad enough that you were cheating on me," she noted, turning around to finally face me. I could see the rage in her reddened eyes as she tried to keep it together. "It's bad enough that you cheated on me with boys." She paused to place her face on her palm. "But you cheated on me with under-aged boys!!!!" She finally let all that rage out. Ting could be quite animated when she wanted to be, but this was well-deserved.

"Ting, I am sorry. I—"

"Sorry? You're *sorry*? Are you sorry? I gave you a chance to come clean and tell me the truth, you didn't! Our daughter is sleeping in the next room! Did you even consider her when you were raping innocent children?" She ranted on, and all I could do was hang my head in shame.

"You're a terrible husband. You are a terrible father." That struck a chord with me. I got angry and glared at her. She just looked at me in astonishment. She couldn't believe I had the gumption to be angry at her right now.

"Oh, did that hurt?" she asked comically, and I just gnashed my teeth. I was not a bad father, and I was not my father. "Are you angry?" she mocked me, and I clenched my fists.

"Watch yourself," I growled.

Ting just looked at me in amusement. I knew I had no right to be angry in a situation like this, but she was treading on thin ice here. I wish I had told her about my father; maybe she would not have poked the bear.

"Are you seriously saying that to me right now, Bat?" she asked in astonishment. "You have no idea. You are a failure as a man, as a human being, as a husband, and definitely as a fath—"

The force of my fist against her face shut her up and sent her staggering backward. How dare she call me my father? Was she mad? Ting just looked at me, a mix of shock and fear in her eyes.

"Are you crazy?" she screamed, but I punched her again, this time in her nose.

Blood gushed out of her nose as she held it with her hands. She tried scurrying to the door, but I got to her, punching her again. She fell on the bed, and I got atop her.

"I am not my father! I am not my father! I am not my father!" I kept reciting as I pressed my hands against her throat, her smaller hands trying to pry mine off to no avail. I kept telling her I was not my father over and over again while strangling her with all my power. For just a split second, I saw my mother before me as I watched the fight in Ting's eyes diminish until her hands fell back on the bed.

When I was done, I laid down beside my wife's dead body. What had I just done? I realized this was exactly how Father killed Mother.

CHAPTER TEN

THE BAT ERDENE WE ALL KNOW AND FEAR

I bent down and inhaled the white substance, rubbing my nose vigorously with my fingers before taking my head upwards to savor the ecstasy. The cocaine ran through my veins and gave me an unbelievable rush. I could feel everyone looking at me, waiting for my reaction. I stabilized myself and looked at them all.

"Let us get this party started!" I screamed at the top of my lungs, and they all roared in unison.

Today was my birthday, and I had invited everyone to my place to celebrate. I had all my guards on the lookout, my new guards. I had fired my former group of guards after Ting told me she had bribed one of them and I...killed her. It had only been a few months since then. I disposed of her body that night and paid off my contacts in the police to block any inquiry into her disappearance. Her family came asking of her after not hearing from her for a while, but I told them she packed her bags and said she was leaving me. They did not believe me at first and even wanted to check the house. I let them because I knew they would not find anything, and they did not. They were still skeptical, so I had my police friends forge documents and files implying she had run off to China. The appearance of such evidence seemed to sway them, and they had no choice but to agree that was what happened. I also told them she took our baby with her and ran away. They went on the wild goose chase while I sat back and relaxed. I sent Shu away to an orphanage and decided I would be paying for her care over there for as long as I lived.

"Happy birthday, sir," Cho, one of the workers in my company, congratulated me, and I patted him on the back.

I walked outside to get some fresh air and saw a few people sitting down and talking. I noticed Ming, sitting on his chair, looking to the stars. I went to meet him. He had not said a word to me since Ting's disappearance.

"Hey, Ming. Why do you look all sad and gloomy?" I always forgot to stop using large words like *gloomy* around him, but it was already a part of me.

I sat down on the pavement opposite him. It was dark, so I couldn't see his face clearly, but the light from the house gave me a vague look at him. Ming remained quiet and just stared at me.

"Ming, are you okay?" I asked cautiously.

"Who are you, sir?" Ming finally asked.

I found that question confusing. What did he mean by that? Did he not know who I was?

"What is the meaning of that?" I asked, partially annoyed at the question.

"Who are you?" he asked again, even bolder than before.

"I am Bat Erdene, of course," I replied, apparently amused at such a question.

"Are you sure?" Ming asked. "Because the Bat Erdene I know would not have killed his wife."

My heart stopped. How did he even know that? Wait, had he known all these months?

"Don't worry, sir." Ming smiled ominously. "I won't tell anyone. I have never betrayed you and never will. Even if I wanted to tell someone, who would I tell? The police? My life would be over."

I calmed down when I heard this. It was good to know he was still loyal to me and not going to spoil it all.

"How did you know?" I asked, not even trying to deny it. I had learned my lesson with Ting not to lie to people I cared about, and regardless of what he thought, I did care about Ming.

"I saw when your men were boarding her into the boot of the car through the window. They probably thought I was sleeping since I didn't come out to open the gate. They opened it themselves and left," Ming explained. "Did you kill her?"

I put my head down and looked at the ground. I didn't want to see his face when I said it.

"Yes, I did."

The silence was what followed my answer. I finally looked up and couldn't believe what I saw. The tears rolled down his eyes as he stared at me, a look of horror, disgust, and fear in his eyes.

"You know," he chimed, "I keep wondering when was the day, the hour, the moment, you became this." He paused to wipe the tears from his face. "Or maybe it was a gradual process...a process to become the Bat Erdene we all know and fear."

I wasn't even angry. The shock of him crying at what I had become still lingered in me. Regardless of what he said, however, I had gone too far, too deep down the rabbit-hole to claw my way out. This was who I was now, and he had to accept it.

"What happened to your daughter, sir?" he asked reluctantly. "Please tell me you did not..." I glared at him when I got what he was trying to imply, and he quickly kept quiet.

"Ming," I said his name after standing up, "believe it or not, you are the only person here I trust. I never have and would never lie to you. I did not kill my daughter. I sent her to an orphanage." I elaborated on the situation with Shu-Chen to Ming.

"That was the best decision you made, sir," Ming said, nodding his head in approval. "The last thing that girl needs is to grow up surrounded by this."

I left Ming and went back inside. What I didn't tell him was I didn't just do it for her but for me as well. That was how selfish and deplorable I had become. I knew without Ting it would be an uphill battle trying to raise

Shu by myself while also enjoying and reveling in who I was now, so I chose myself over her.

I went back in and looked around. People were giving in to their carnal desires without fear of judgment by society. Men and women engaging in sexual pleasures, people trying new things like cocaine and what they call *weed*. If I had remained weighed down by dead weight like family or work, I would not have been elucidated to the real joys of life. I saw two women waving at me at the end of the hallway before walking toward me.

"Hello, Mr. Erdene," the plumper of the two women said.

"Oh please, call me Bat Erdene," I instructed, waving my hand dismissively in the air. "What can I do for you?" I was partially high on cocaine, which made me in a more accommodating state to strangers.

"I am Nomin," she began. "I was the one who wrote you about a business offer you might be interested in."

"Oh, it's you," I exclaimed, guiding them to a secluded part of the house where we could talk in private. "I am interested in what you are proposing. I assume you have the means of acquiring these girls you speak of."

Nomin nodded.

"This is Tula," she gestured toward the other woman, who smiled at me. She had a disarming look to her which I thought would come in handy when she tries to convince girls to follow her into the business. "I would propose she handle the recruitment at Chiang Rai since she knows the area and people very well, including law enforcement."

I turned and looked at her in surprise. Such an unassuming-looking lady was this corrupt. A smile crept across my mouth in amusement.

"Do you?" I asked Tula.

"I do," she said with a charming smile. She only spoke when it was her turn. She knew the chain of command. I was impressed.

"All right," I agreed, much to their surprise. "I'm in. I will give you all the money you need to work for me in bringing these girls to become prostitutes for clients. I will use my vast resources to advertise to my lucrative friends whom I know discretely are interested. You will both be given a share of the profits monthly based on how much we generate."

This was not really a negotiation to me since they needed me more than I needed them. They would have to take it or leave it, but if they left it, I could easily do it by myself thanks to them; they had given me the idea.

"And let me just make this clear. If you agree to this, it will not be a partnership of any kind. You will work for me," I growled, moving closer to them in a bid at intimidating them, which seemed to work.

The two women both looked at each other, with Tula nodding at Nomin.

"We accept, Bat Erdene," Nomin said, and I smiled.

"Good," I surmised, resting back in my chair. "You can both leave. Go, enjoy the party, we will talk later."

Both women stood and proceeded to leave.

"Wait," I said just as they reached the door, and they both stopped on their tracks. "This house will be the headquarters of all operations." They both looked shocked at my declaration. "Is that clear?"

"Yes, Bat Erdene," Nomin said.

I waved them away prior to both of them exiting the room. After they left, I pondered on what this new business would mean. My construction company was going down the drain, no thanks to me. It felt like I wanted it to be done for because it was basically my father's, not mine. My wife was dead. My daughter was gone. I had nothing that was mine...nothing except this house, this building, this symbol. I would make it a haven for people to enact their greatest desires, perversions, and pleasures. After Ting's death, I returned to my schedule with the boys, but going to hotels was not enough. I would start bringing them home. I would turn this place into an extension of my life at the moment. Freedom, drugs, sex, parties, and joy.

Maybe all these would fill that void I have had ever since my mother died. Perhaps they would accommodate for the lack of a soul I have. Maybe, just maybe, I could still be happy. I got up from my seat, walking out into the new life I had promised myself.

CHAPTER ELEVEN

An Odd Encounter

I shut down Erdene Constructions a year after my meeting with Nomin and Tula, but we had started the prostitution business much earlier. I contacted my friends and notified them about the new establishment I was forming in different parts of China and even Bangkok. I made establishments in Beijing, Shanghai, Chiang Rai, Zhengzhou, and others. Over the years we had attracted a lot of traffic from clients, especially rich ones. I had learned over the years and tapered all the cracks of the business in a bid to make it run as flawlessly as possible.

I usually went on check-ups to each establishment to see how it was faring and if the money I pumped in was actually being used for what I expected. It had been seven years now since Nomin made the pitch to me and I was with her at Zhengzhou to check up on the brothel I had made in that region. I was relaxing and drinking in the living room when I saw Nomin ready to go out.

"Where are you off to?" I asked her, placing my glass on the table and glancing in her direction.

"I have to go and meet Nugai to receive the new intake of girls," she explained, and I nodded, waving her away.

I thought about relaxing here but it was pretty boring with no one to amuse me and few people to talk to, so I decided to go with her.

"Wait," I beckoned as she was about to leave the door, and she stopped, turning to look at me.

"What do you need, Bat Erdene?"

I always found it weird that she constantly called me by my full name. However, I knew it was out of respect, so I did not worry about it too much.

"I am going to follow you," I said calmly while standing up.

"Why, if I may ask?" Nomin asked. She probably felt I did not trust her, which made her a bit unhappy. I did not trust her, but that was not why I was following her.

"Don't worry, Nomin," I assured, placing a hand on her shoulder. "I am just bored, let us go."

We drove in quiet through the road as I took in the unenviable scenery of Zhengzhou. It was obvious from the quality of the infrastructure that this place was below par, probably housing lowlife and people living in squalor. I spat on the ground as we drove by, looking at impoverished vagabonds and rascals trying to make ends meet. This, though, was what made Zhengzhou an ideal place for the kind of business we conducted. Law enforcement was weak and malleable, and the population was ravaged by low-income earners, making it easier to bribe parents into selling their children. We finally arrived at the outskirts of the city and stopped in front of a truck. Nomin and I both came down to check on the merchandise. We were guided to a room and entered it, sitting on the chairs that were provided for us. A couple of moments after, the girls were brought in so we could inspect them.

I looked at the girls, scouring through the litany of scared and timid faces. Their lives had already been hell before coming here. I was doing them a favor, and they should have been grateful. I smiled at them and they shivered, retreating as far away from me as possible. They also smelled, but that was to be expected since some of them had been transported in tight spaces for days. What they did not understand as young girls were that, life was awful and unfair. Their lives were never going to be better than what it was now, so better they used that to serve me and still be fed and clothed. Some of these girls did not even have three square meals daily, and yet I was willing to give them that as well as meetings with influential men, one of which could take them away to foreign lands. They should have been bloody grateful. I noticed an immensely attractive girl among them. I immediately knew she would be a catch for certain clients who liked beautiful girls. Nomin had stood up to converse with a man I did not know nor cared to.

"What's he doing here?" I heard Nomin say and furrowed my brows.

A boy? Here? Why? I quickly whipped my head to Nomin and the man she was talking to. I think she called him Nugan or Nugai.

"We found him and these two girls in the desert," the man explained the situation.

I took a good look at the boy. He was moderately built, looking like he was in his early teens, but what really caught me were his eyes. I could see the conviction in them, a conviction I once had. I decided there and then that it would be great to break him and make him submit. Turn him into my new plaything. I could see two girls close to him, frowning as well.

"The boy looks like trouble. He escaped from his initial captors. Don't worry, he's not for you. Someone would find a world for him here in China," the man continued, looking at me this time. No one was taking him but me.

"I will take him," I said authoritatively to the man then turned to the boy with a smile.

He was looking at me. I hoped my smile would make him less abrasive. Nomin looked at me, shocked.

"Bat Erdene," she began, "you are not staying long in China. You will be going back to Bangkok any moment from now. Don't you think the boy will be too much trouble for you?"

I looked at her, surprised that she had spoken out of turn.

"I'm still around, and I will have the boy," I commanded. "And that's final!"

Nomin and the other man agreed with me. I promptly turned to leave the room but was called upon by the boy.

"Sir," he called, even stepping forth toward me. I turned and glanced at him, wondering what could give him the grit to call me as I was leaving. He kept pointing at the two girls I had noticed with him earlier. All three of them were crying. Were they related or something? "I was taken from home with my two sisters—Altantsetseg and Chinua—and my brother, Khulan. Khulan...he is not here. He was shot in the desert and I...I left him to die, sir. Please, if you take me, also take my sisters with you. Don't keep us far from each other. They are already broken, sir. Please. Please. I will do anything."

By the time he was done, he had crawled to my feet, his sobs the only pauses to his monologue. I looked over at the girls and saw the fear in their faces. I found this display of humility worthy of being granted.

I still needed to be sure they were worth it business-wise, not just because my new toy begged it. I walked past the boy to his two sisters, rubbing their hair against my palm. I parted the hair so I could get a good look at the girls. They were moderately pretty and had long hair, but most of all, they seemed determined. I knew that day they would be among the ones to last long in this business and maybe even make it out. I sighed and looked to Nomin.

"Have them washed, Nomin," I instructed. "I will be back in an hour."

"Yes, sir," she replied as I began walking away.

Wait! I almost forgot about the stunning girl that had me enthralled at the beginning.

"Oh! I almost forgot," I mused, walking over to the pretty but shy girl who had been looking down most of the time. She was the opposite of the other two girls. She had an abundance of beauty but none of their zeal and spunk. "What is your name, beautiful girl?" I asked in a nice and charming tone.

"Qara," she replied timidly.

"Qara, you are coming with me, too," I told her before strolling out of the room. I gestured at the man with Nomin to come over and he almost sprinted at my call.

"Come with me. These are your wares. Let me know how much you are taking for each of them, especially the boy!" I instructed prior to opening the curtain. Of course, the boy was my priority. Every other thing was just a bonus.

"Make sure they bathe, Nomin. They smell like pigs!" I ordered Nomin before leaving.

We drove back to the establishment at Zhengzhou with Ming opening the gate. I always took Ming with me to all the establishments since I had started it seven years ago. He already knew whom I had become and still decided to stand by me and never betray me, even though he did not agree with my lifestyle. That was why I trusted him wholeheartedly. He was the only one I trusted without reserve. I came down from the car after we had parked and immediately went over to Ming, completely forgetting about the new merchandise I had procured.

"New recruits?" he asked sarcastically. I knew he was not pleased every time I brought children to become prostitutes, which was why I was so impressed that he remained loyal to me.

"Come on, Ming, don't be like this," I urged with a smile.

"I am not being like anything, sir," he replied with a smile. "I just wanted to know if we had new children to use as prostitutes, and is that a boy?" He bent his neck in an attempt to see if he was correct in his assessment.

"Yes, it is a boy," I replied, rolling my eyes.

He widened his eyes and gave me an *are you serious* look.

"Don't judge, okay," I said, and he sighed. "I need to have my fun. I need a plaything."

"But that boy is not a plaything," he also noted. "He is a human being with dreams, aspirations and a family."

"His life will not get better than this. I am helping him. He might be dead before thirty or kidnapped for much worse or live a wretched life in poverty." Ming just shrugged. "Relax, Ming. It's all good."

I proceeded into the building and chose to see how the girls were faring. When I reached the hallway, I could see Zheng, my lead bodyguard, walking over to the two girls. I figured they had already provoked him, and Zheng was known to be short-fused. However, I also considered they were young and new to all this. He had to be patient and give them the benefit of the doubt that they would learn. They should have at least a day to acclimate to their new environment.

"Zheng!" I called, and all four of them looked at my direction.

"The little girl can put up with her sister for only today, can she not, Zheng?" I said, looking into his eyes and smiling.

Zheng finally calmed down, which was what I wanted. I loved showing him and newcomers who were the boss, so they would not get things twisted. There was a chain of command, and I sat at the top.

"If you say so, Bat Erdene," Zheng submitted, and my smile widened.

"Then let it be so," I concluded. I moved over to the two girls, bringing out a knife from my pocket. I wiggled it before one of the girls' face.

"What is this, my angel?" I asked in a nice tone.

She remained silent. This annoyed me, and she sure did not want to see me when I was annoyed.

"What is this?" I raised my voice, asking her again.

"A knife," she answered, and I smiled. She had to learn to obey, they both did.

"Good girl." I felt her soft, long hair again as I stared into her eyes. "Today will be the last time you sleep in your sister's room. If you ever create drama like this again, this knife will surely be for your sister's head. Understand?" I explained as clearly as possible, so she could understand me clearly.

"Yes," she answered, obviously rattled from what I said.

I stood up and told the boy to follow me.

I took the boy to my room and inspected him. He was to be my new plaything now, no questions asked. I had sex with him and it was also then I finally knew his name, Od. Other than the occasional shouts Od had at night calling the name of someone named Yuna, I slept like a baby that night with my *toy* lying on the ground and sleeping there. The next morning, I told him to clean himself up since he was bleeding. The look in his eyes, eyes filled with despair and fear, was all I needed that morning to know it was going to be a good day. I was shocked that he wanted to even go out and explained to him he was to remain in this room until I said so, no one else was allowed to touch what I had claimed as mine.

When I left, on my way out, I saw Zheng.

"Give him food regularly," I ordered. "I don't want him skinny for when I want to have my way with him."

Zheng nodded before I left. I knew Od was fearless, and that was what I loved about him the most, and what would make it all the sweeter breaking him. I went to do some humanitarian work and came back that night in a good mood. I tied Od up and flogged him mercilessly, insulting him as I did so. This was what pleasure felt like. This was true bliss, free of judgment.

I continued my routine with Od for a few years. I went to other parts on business and when I came back, there was always Od to whip and use the way I saw fit. He kept calling that Yuna person, though, and I had begun flogging him for it. He later told me it was his mother, so I let it slide a little bit, only flogging him when it really bothered me.

One faithful morning, I got home from a short business trip, spoke with Ming lightly before going in, and went to my room, ready to see my pet. I had bought him snapdragon flowers, which Ting had loved so much. When I entered my room, I saw Od sleeping and smiled. He woke up and saw me but didn't move an inch. I walked over to him and handed him the flowers.

"For you," I said. "My wife loved flowers."

I watched as Od accepted them from me and placed them on the table. He had really grown over the years. His English had improved, and he had even learned some of my mannerisms. I had brought him to just be a plaything I could use until I got bored, but he had so much potential, potential that was being wasted. I smelled something, a scent, a strange scent. I sniffed over and over again until I confirmed someone other than me had been here.

"Od, was someone in this room when I was away?"

"Yes, Bat Erdene. A white man was here," Od explained. "Zheng brought him in. He said he's your man."

What did I just hear? Zheng brought a stranger to my room...to do what? Have sex with my property? Steal?

"He's my man? He's my man? He's not my fucking man!" I shouted in anger. "I have to teach that bastard a final lesson."

I stormed out of the room and locked the door. I briskly walked downstairs, bringing out the gun I carried with me. I saw Zheng in the living room giving orders to some men.

"Zheng!" I called, and he turned to look at me. I pointed the gun at him, and he tried to run out, but I motioned to the guards to block his path, and they did.

"You fucking brought a stranger into my establishment?!" I screamed. "You took him to my room! For fucking what?"

His hands were up in the air, and I could see his fear of death.

"Answer me!" I shouted, which shook him.

"I...I brought him to have sex with your boy...so I could get some e-ext...tra cash," he stammered.

I had already suspected this, but it was still shocking to actually hear him say it.

"You what?"

"I'm sor—" The bullet in his brain prevented him from saying any more.

I turned around, looking at everyone.

"Clean this shit up," I ordered before storming back to my room. I smiled as I walked. Now that was a true message I had just sent. They would learn that no one was above me. Anyone who got too big-headed would meet the same fate as Zheng. I unlocked and opened the door, entering inside to see Od, who was shocked at my suddenly calm disposition. I had done what I wanted. I was still in control.

CHAPTER TWELVE

ESCAPE FROM ERDENE

On the third year of having Od as my pet, an unusual incident happened. It was early in the morning, and I was indulging in a little bit of cocaine and alcohol with my plaything, Od, in bed when I heard a loud scream. I immediately sprang up from my bed, boarded my slippers with my feet and sprinted out of the room, forgetting to lock it. I met one of my guards, Chow, on the way.

"What the hell is going on, Chow?" I demanded.

"There has been...an occurrence, sir," he said.

I looked at him, expecting him to explain, but all he did was look at me. It seemed he was unsure on how to go about it. I groaned, letting him lead me to the source of the issue.

"This better be worth it," I warned, "or you and the screamer will pay with your heads."

We reached the room, and I got inside. My eyes widened in disbelief. The most beautiful girl in the establishment, Qara, was hanging and slightly dangling on a rope. She was undoubtedly dead. Her beautiful black locks rolled down, covering parts of her face, but not the mouth. Her tongue stuck out of her mouth. I wasn't sure if she did that on purpose or if it was a reflex of her reaction to the struggle of being hanged. From the looks of it, she also hanged herself. I walked over to her closely while fighting off the tears. My men could not see me cry or be sad here. I remembered the day I saw her and knew she might not be cut out for this line of work. I took her nonetheless based on my selfish lure to her beauty, and now this poor girl was dead...dead because of me. I shifted the hair on her face to take a look at her eyes. They were half-open, the sadness so evident in her irises. She had really given up.

"Take her out of here," I ordered after turning to address the men. "We'll go bury her somewhere before she spoils the market and makes today's work hard."

Some of them and most of the girls looked shocked at my callous handling of the matter, but that was the point. They had to fear me and think I had no emotions.

"And let this be a lesson to the rest of you," I cautioned, waggling my finger in the air. "Any of you try this shit, this is how you will be buried, and business will continue as usual. Everybody is expendable."

I promptly left. I walked in despair to my downstairs as I thought about how I just shat on that poor girl's memory. Would she have been better if I had left her to her previous life? It was pointless thinking about that now. I got to the living room to check that everything was still in order and spent a few minutes overseeing the carrying of Qara's body from her room to the car that would take her away. I walked in defeat to my room with sunken shoulders, head faced down and back arched downward. I finally entered my room and saw Od by the window. I remembered they were next to each other when I picked them both, so he probably knew the girl. I could see the sadness in his face as he turned to look at me. I closed the door, trying to find the words to explain to him what had just happened.

"A girl...a girl was sick," I began. "She fainted. That's why you heard that scream." I lied. I wanted to ease his pain. It would do him no good to know she killed herself.

Od remained silent. I knew there was nothing I could say to make him feel better, so I just sighed and headed to my wardrobe to get a change of clothes. I changed and left quietly, getting into my car and being driven out of the compound. On the way, my eyes made contact with Ming, who had opened the gate for me. I could see the pain and disappointment in his eyes. I wondered how many times I would disappoint him before he finally snapped. I had already disappointed everyone I had cared about, so it was not something new to me. We drove until we arrived at a secluded spot at the outskirts of the city. I made them bury her next to the flowers and made sure they later made a tombstone for her with the engraving: Here Lies Qara, Loving Daughter and Friend. It wasn't much, but it was the best I could do for her in a lame attempt to try and honor her memory.

I didn't go back to the house that night. I wandered around the city and saw how it looked like for the first time that night. If there was one thing Zhengzhou had, it was culture. Several local dances on the streets, some of which I took part in, and a couple of local games, all of which I failed, were just some of the pleasures I enjoyed that night. I was having such a good time I decided to sleep in a hotel. That night, I thought about a lot of things: Father, Mother, Ming, Ting, Shu and even Od. The poor boy's eyes and face when he found out Qara, his friend, had died, haunted me throughout the night. What I was doing to him was not right. What if he killed himself, too? These things ran through my mind, and I surmised I would take him with me to Bangkok when I traveled the next day.

The next day, I ordered Od and his two sisters go with me to Bangkok. They all packed their things, and we left along with Ming, of course.

In Bangkok, I stopped having sex with Od. I think the incident with Qara made me have a soft spot for him and pity him. I even gave him more freedom to do what he wanted. I had started my drug business much later than I did the prostitution, but it had already been booming in just a few years. I still had my sexual needs, so I found a ridiculously beautiful eleven-year-old Colombian boy to be my new pet. It seemed the talent ran in the family because his sister was also an amazing dancer with unique moves, bringing her exotic Colombian style to attract more customers to our establishment. I named my pet *The Beautiful* because he was just so beautiful, and I believed everyone agreed he was unbelievably beautiful.

Slowly but surely, I began to ask more of Od and hand him more responsibility in the house. He had not given me a reason yet to think he was unable to handle it and I had broken him over the years. I had trouble trusting the rest of my guards ever since Zheng, so I was forced to place some of the load on Od. Chai was still in charge of the guards in Bangkok, however. He was big and fearful, and some people surprisingly thought he was equal to me. I laughed at this notion, for even Chai himself knew I could kill him whenever I wanted.

Eventually, I found out Od might not be trusted after all. His sister, who had become one of the main attractions of the years, suddenly went missing. I had arrived back from a trip when I was informed of this, and I was livid. Altantsetseg was the girl that brought in the highest revenue, followed by her and Od's sister, Chinua. I sent for Od, asking him where the bitch was, but he was proving to be smart. What he didn't know was I knew he had become friends with Gabriel, my pet. The two animals were probably bonding over their mutual experience as my playthings, which amused me, but now, I was definitely not amused. I quickly went to my room and dragged Gabriel out, bringing him before Od. To my surprise, Od still didn't budge. I was almost impressed. I eventually killed Th Beautiful as punishment to Od. He would know he killed the innocent boy.

Eventually, Tula sent two troublesome girls she said would be better suited here. I had enough issues as it was in Bangkok, but I accepted them nonetheless. She said their names were Yuna and Cyril. I remembered the name Yuna in particular because she shared the same name as Od's mother. I went to see them when they first arrived. I saw the same fire I saw in Od's eyes in this Yuna girl and was immediately interested in her. Over the following months, business went on as smoothly as possible. The new girls learned the routes with which to sell drugs and the prostitutes did their thing.

A couple of months later, Chai was shot dead. I didn't really care, but it was what came next that truly unnerved me.

I was having a drink in the living room when Batu approached me.

"What is it this time, Batu?" I asked, already bored by his presence.

"Od has escaped with Chinua, Cyril, Gabriella, and Yuna!" he exclaimed, and I jumped from my seat.

"What did you just fucking say?"

I hoped I had misheard him. He repeated what he just said and I ran outside. I wanted to go on a tirade and send for men to scour all the ends of the country to find them. Then I saw Ming, sitting in his signature chair, staring at me. Then, for some reason, I just knew. Was it really worth it? Didn't they deserve a life better than this one after earning me so much money? Should they be under my care forever? Ming and I smiled at each other simultaneously

"Sir...sir, what do we do?!" Batu asked, apparently in a panic.

I looked up at the sky.

"Nothing," I stated calmly.

"Did you just say 'nothing,' sir?" Batu asked, not believing what he had just heard.

"Yes," I replied. "Those brave enough to dare to dream should be allowed to live the dream."

For some inexplicable reason, I was happy for them. They were free, yet I was still a prisoner of my needs and fears. Some people deserve to be happy. They made the right choices at the right moments, even though I did not.

''Word-of-mouth is crucial for any author to succeed.

If you enjoyed the book, please leave a review on my Amazon review page, even if it is just a sentence or two. It would make all the difference''

Gangs of Stockholm - A Fallen Angel

Get Your Hands on This E-Book & Find Out Today!

If you would like to sign up for my newsletter, please visit www.cedenheim.com

Made in the
USA
Middletown, DE